New Frontiers in Translation Studies

SpringerBriefs in Empirical Translation Modelling

Empirical translation has become a mainstream research branch in translation studies in recent years with the rise of empiricism in the humanities and the social sciences in Europe at the turn of the twenty-first century. It is an interdisciplinary, methodologically oriented research paradigm which seeks to explore language and textual patterns in translations in relation to the source language and texts or the original target language. Language corpora or digital text collections provide the essential research resources for empirical translation. As a result, empirical translation and corpus translation have been used as largely exchangeable concepts. With the increasing availability of large quantities of web-based natural language and translation resources, there is a growing trend to introduce data science methods to empirical translation research, which has been mainly using statistics to explore linguistic and textual patterns in translations. This new Springer Briefs series will usher in a new period of disciplinary development in empirical translation studies by introducing data science methods and techniques in the study of a wide range of translation genres, products, services, and social activities. Empirical translation modelling refers to both the statistical and computational modelling of translations and related language and text materials, as well as related societal and human behavioural patterns and events. This new series aims to provoke academic debates among scholars of translation studies and cognate fields such as linguistics, computer science, natural language processing, statistics the feasibility and productivity of using statistics and machine learning methods to advance translation research ranging from translation quality assessment, translation technology evaluation to healthcare and health risk translation and communication, and global policy translation such as social and environmental sustainability and social equality. This new series is visionary and pioneering for both its focus on research methodological innovation and the broader research agenda it aims to develop for empirical translation studies. Titles in this series will illustrate important social, environmental contributions that empirical translation research can and will make to more sustainable and equitable social development around the world.

Yi Shan · Meng Ji

Cultural Adaptation in Chinese Mental Health Translation

 Springer

Yi Shan
College of International Studies,
Jiaxing University
Jiaxing, China

Meng Ji
School of Languages and Cultures
The University of Sydney
Sydney, NSW, Australia

ISSN 2197-8689 ISSN 2197-8697 (electronic)
New Frontiers in Translation Studies
ISSN 2731-0515 ISSN 2731-0523 (electronic)
SpringerBriefs in Empirical Translation Modelling
ISBN 978-981-97-1726-2 ISBN 978-981-97-1727-9 (eBook)
https://doi.org/10.1007/978-981-97-1727-9

© The Author(s) 2024. This book is an open access publication.

Open Access This book is licensed under the terms of the Creative Commons Attribution-NonCommercial-NoDerivatives 4.0 International License (http://creativecommons.org/licenses/by-nc-nd/4.0/), which permits any noncommercial use, sharing, distribution and reproduction in any medium or format, as long as you give appropriate credit to the original author(s) and the source, provide a link to the Creative Commons license and indicate if you modified the licensed material. You do not have permission under this license to share adapted material derived from this book or parts of it.

The images or other third party material in this book are included in the book's Creative Commons license, unless indicated otherwise in a credit line to the material. If material is not included in the book's Creative Commons license and your intended use is not permitted by statutory regulation or exceeds the permitted use, you will need to obtain permission directly from the copyright holder.

This work is subject to copyright. All commercial rights are reserved by the author(s), whether the whole or part of the material is concerned, specifically the rights of translation, reprinting, reuse of illustrations, recitation, broadcasting, reproduction on microfilms or in any other physical way, and transmission or information storage and retrieval, electronic adaptation, computer software, or by similar or dissimilar methodology now known or hereafter developed. Regarding these commercial rights a non-exclusive license has been granted to the publisher.

The use of general descriptive names, registered names, trademarks, service marks, etc. in this publication does not imply, even in the absence of a specific statement, that such names are exempt from the relevant protective laws and regulations and therefore free for general use.

The publisher, the authors and the editors are safe to assume that the advice and information in this book are believed to be true and accurate at the date of publication. Neither the publisher nor the authors or the editors give a warranty, expressed or implied, with respect to the material contained herein or for any errors or omissions that may have been made. The publisher remains neutral with regard to jurisdictional claims in published maps and institutional affiliations.

This Springer imprint is published by the registered company Springer Nature Singapore Pte Ltd.
The registered company address is: 152 Beach Road, #21-01/04 Gateway East, Singapore 189721, Singapore

Paper in this product is recyclable.

Preface

Demonic possession, insanity, character weakness, illness, or disability—what is your perception of mental disorders? How do you call them in your language? From highly stigmatizing and negative to increasingly linguistically and culturally neutral and inclusive, the naming of mental health conditions in English has been and continues to be evolving in the last 150 years, driven by medical research and increasing international awareness of the human rights of people with lived experience. In 1952, the American Psychiatric Association (APA) published the internationally authoritative *Diagnostic and Statistical Manual of Mental Disorders* (DSM-I). Since then, the APA has updated the DSM five times. Earlier discriminatory mental health names like 'manic-depressive illness', 'alcoholism', 'drug addiction', 'paranoid personality', and 'hysterical personality' in DSM-II (1968) were redesigned and replaced in DSM-V (2013) by more neutral or less stigmatizing names: 'bipolar disorder', 'alcohol use disorder', 'substance use disorder', 'delusional disorder', and 'histrionic personality disorder'. Some highly discriminatory names in DSM-I (1952) and DSM-II (1968) such as 'mental retardation', 'homosexuality', 'senile dementia', 'alcoholic paranoia' were entirely removed in DSM-IV (1994) and DSM-V (2013) (Boller & Forbes, 1998; Drescher, 2015; Harris, 2013).

A 2019 report by the World Health Organization 'Advocacy for Mental Health, Disability, and Human Rights' called on international societies to create a more inclusive environment for people with disabilities caused by mental health conditions. The WHO report, endorsed by medical specialists, mental health organizations and human rights advocacies in over 30 countries, represents an international effort to destigmatize mental health conditions and protect the human rights of people diagnosed with a mental health condition. International efforts to create a more inclusive social environment for people with mental health conditions are echoed in new national mental health language guidelines. In Australia, the Mental Health Complaints Commissioner (MHCC), established under the Mental Health Act 2014, requires that terms such as 'mental illnesses, diseases, and burdens' be replaced with more inclusive terms such as 'mental health conditions, challenges, and impact' to illustrate the underlying principle of re-designing mental health terms by putting the impact of mental disorders on people with lived experience, their practical needs, and their everyday life challenges and feelings, first and above all (MHCC Language Guide, 2020).

Naming of health conditions is the building block of health research (Brown, 1995). It also provides a critical entry point for the public to understand health concepts and notions in their own language and culture (Clegg, 2012; Kingdon et al., 2013). Different countries have different mental healthcare systems, thus distinct mental health terminologies in national languages. Nevertheless, a common term base of key mental health terms, particularly, the names of mental health conditions, provides the foundation for international health research and public communication. Translation plays an instrumental role in bridging the language and cultural gaps in the development of international scientific terminology (Bower, 2015; Cabré, 2010). The ongoing design of mental health condition names in English, illustrated by the five editions of the DSM since 1952, has had and will continue to have an important impact on the re-conceptualization and communication of mental health conditions in other languages and cultures (see Kochhar et al., 2007, on translating DSM-IV to Indian languages including Bengali, Hindi, Gujarati, Tamil, Telugu, and Urdu; Binde & Forsström, 2015; Boeschoten et al., 2018; Castrén et al., 2014; Ibrahim et al., 2018, Þórðarson et al., 2020; Sato & Takahashi, 2016, on translating DSM-V to Finnish, Swedish, Japanese, Dutch, Arabic, and Icelandic).

Another critical, yet understudied role of health condition name translation is to inform the design of condition names in English, and possible replacement of existing stigmatizing mental health condition names. Maruta and Matsumoto (2018) reported that in 1996, on the ground that 'the term Seishin-Bunretsu-Byo is humiliating', the Japanese Society for Psychiatry and Neurology replaced the literal translation of Schizophrenia 'Seishin-Bunretsu-Byo' ('mind splitting disease' 精神分裂病) with 'Togo-Shitcho-Sho' ('disintegration disorder' 統合失調症). The revised Japanese translation utilized two more neutral kanji-based morphemes to destigmatize the English name: the prefix Schizo- (split) was replaced by Shitcho (失調) (lack of coordination); the suffix -phrenia (disordered mind) was changed to Togo (統合) (integration, in this context, one's ability to integrate and coordinate different brain functions). Sartorius et al. (2014) reported that within 7 months of the official approval of the new translation, 78% of psychiatric practices in Japan used the new translation. An early effect of renaming Schizophrenia was that people who agreed to be diagnosed with the condition doubled in two years, from 36.7% in 2002 to 69.7% in 2004 (n = 1944). The renaming of Schizophrenia via a culturally more inclusive, less stigmatizing translation improved the access to mental health services for Japanese people who would otherwise be humiliated by the diagnosis. The reinvention of the name of Schizophrenia in Japan prompted international efforts in the next two decades to consider alternative names of Schizophrenia (Henderson & Malhi, 2014; Keshevan et al., 2011; Levin, 2006; Murray, 2006). The redesign of its translation in East Asian countries sharing similar traditional cultures with Japan (South Korea, Taiwan, and Hong Kong) reported similar positive social effects (Chiu et al., 2021; Lasalvia et al., 2015). Internationally, consensus has not been reached to replace Schizophrenia, which remains in DSM-V (2013) as a major spectrum of psychotic disorders.

Preface

Mental disorders have developed different socio-psychological properties in different cultures (Corrigan & Rao, 2012). By 1880, seven categories of mental health conditions were distinguished in Europe: mania, melancholia, monomania, paresis, dementia, dipsomania, and epilepsy (Gonaver, 2019). According to Lin (1981), traditional Chinese culture classifies *Tien-K'uang* 癲狂 (craziness, psychoses) into *Tien* 癲 (apathetic), *Hsien* 癇 (epilepsy), *K'uang* 狂 (agitated), *Ch'ih* 痴 (hypomanic excitement), *Yü* 鬱 (depressed), and *Tsao* 躁 (manic). Despite the linguistic and cultural distance between English and Chinese, their naming traditions of mental health conditions share the use of linguistic elements that can induce stigmatizing perceptions of mental disorders. These include culturally negative suffixes, pre-fixes in English of Greek or Latin origins, and stigmatizing characters as basic lexical units in Chinese traditional mental health cultures: -mania (μανία) (狂, 躁 *kuáng, zào*), -lepsis (λεψις) (癇 *xián*), -phobia (φοβία) (-懼 *jù*), and dipsa- (δίψα) (酗 *xù*).

Functional translation primarily concerns with achieving culturally more neutral understanding and perceptions of mental disorders among the target readers. A functional, inclusive translation requires not merely a replacement of negative English suffixes, prefixes, and adjectives that induce the use of negative Chinese characters, but a more holistic approach which conveys the underlying meaning or the essence of a mental disorder, using culturally neutral, less stigmatizing Mandarin Chinese characters. In this process, linguistic dependence on the source language is carefully controlled: Higher dependence is preserved when the translation is sensible and sensitive in the target culture; greater independence, including the use of alternative English expressions of similar meaning but higher cross-cultural translatability, is exercised, when the literal translation can cause potential misunderstanding that perpetuates stigma of mental disorders.

In this book, we propose a culturally inclusive, comprehensible, and appropriate approach to the translation of terms and expressions to Mandarin Chinese. We will use examples to illustrate how culturally inclusive translation can influence the perceptions of mental disorders by the target audiences. In this process, translators should bear in mind that translations which evoke associations with insanity and character weakness must be avoided.

Diseases with underlying insane characters or character weaknesses must be avoided: Current medical knowledge of mental disorders is very limited (Fried, 2022). Mental disorders are much more complex than somatic diseases (Malla et al., 2015). Stigmatization can create unnecessary psychological barriers for people to access mental health services, especially in developing countries (Gómez-Restrepo et al., 2021).

Mental disorders, which offer more neutral descriptions and interpretations of mental health conditions and their associated difficulties for people, are encouraged. Sanderson and Andrew (2002) discussed the results of the Australian National Survey of Mental Health and Well-being, based on a survey of 10,641 adults to demonstrate that the use of mental disorders evokes others' understanding, support of people with mental disorders, and a more inclusive social and cultural environment in general.

Sydney, Australia Meng Ji
Shanghai, China Yi Shan
September 2023

References

Bassnett, S. (2011). The translator as cross-cultural mediator. In K. Malmkjær, & K. Windle (Eds.) *The Oxford handbook of translation studies*. Oxford Academic, Sept 18 2012. https://doi.org/10.1093/oxfordhb/9780199239306.013.0008

Binde, P., & Forsström, D. (2015). The Swedish translation of DSM-5 "Gambling Disorder": Reflections on nosology and terminology. *Nordic Studies on Alcohol and Drugs, 32*(2), 219–222.

Boller, F., & Forbes, M. (1998). History of dementia and dementia in history. *Journal of the Neurological Sciences, 158*(2), 125–133.

Bower, L. (2015) Terminology and translation. In H. J. Kockaert, F. Steurs, & John Benjamins (Eds.), *Handbook of terminology*.

Brown, P. (1995). Naming and framing: The social construction of diagnosis and illness. *Journal of Health & Social Behavior*, 34–52.

Cabré, M. T. (2010). Terminology and translation. In L. van Doorslaer (Ed.), *Handbook of translation studies*. John Benjamins.

Chiu, Y. H., et al. (2021). Effects of renaming Schizophrenia on destigmatization among medical students in One Taiwan University. *International Journal of Environmental Research and Public Health, 18*(17), 9347.

Clegg, J. W. (2012). Teaching about mental health and illness through the history of the DSM. *History of Psychology, 15*(4), 364–370.

Colina, S. (2008). Translation quality evaluation: Empirical evidence for a functionalist approach. *The Translator, 14*(1), 97–134.

Colina, S. (2015). *Fundamentals of translation*. Cambridge University Press.

Corrigan, P. W., & Rao, D. (2012). On the self-stigma of mental illness. *The Canadian Journal of Psychiatry, 57*(8), 464–469.

Drescher J. (2015). Out of DSM: Depathologizing homosexuality. *Behavioral Sciences, 5*(4), 565–575.

Fried, E. I. (2022). Studying mental health problems as systems, not syndromes. *Current Directions in Psychological Science, 31*(6), 500–508.

Gómez-Restrepo, C., et al. (2021). Access barriers, self-recognition, and recognition of depression and unhealthy alcohol use: A qualitative study. *Revista Colombiana de Psiquiatria, 50*(Suppl 1), 52–63.

Gonaver, W. (2019). *The peculiar institution and the making of modern psychiatry, 1840–1880*. University of North Carolina Press.

Harris, J. C. (2013). New terminology for mental retardation in DSM-5 and ICD-11. *Current Opinion in Psychiatry, 26*(3), 260–262.

Henderson, S., & Malhi, G.S. (2014) Swan song for schizophrenia? *The Australian and New Zealand Journal of Psychiatry, 48*, 302–305.

Jensen, M. N. (2015). Optimising comprehensibility in interlingual translation. In Maksymski et al. (Eds.), *Translation and comprehensibility* (Vol. 72, pp. 163–194). Frank & Timme GmbH.

Ji, M. (2013a). *Quantitative exploration of historical translations: A study of Tetsugaku Jii* (哲學字彙). RAM-Verlag.

Ji, M. (2013b). *A corpus-based study of historical Chinese lexis*. Waseda University Press.

Ji, M. (2019) (ed.) *Cross-cultural health translation: Exploring methodological and digital tools*. Routledge.

Kato, T., & Takahashi, S. (2016). Evolving DSM and its Japanese translation. In *Psychiatry and clinical neurosciences, 70*(9), 369–370.

Keshavan MS, et al. (2011) Schizophrenia: moving ahead with the schizophrenia concept. In *Schizophrenia Research, 127*, 3–13.

Kim, S., et al. (2021). Development and psychometric evaluation of the Dementia Public Stigma Scale. *International Journal of Geriatric Psychiatry*, 37(2). https://doi.org/10.1002/gps.5672

Kingdon, D., et al. (2013). Changing name: Changing prospects for psychosis. *Epidemiology and Psychiatric Sciences, 22*(4), 297–301.

Kochhar, P. H., Rajadhyaksha, S. S., & Suvarna, V. R. (2007). Translation and validation of brief patient health questionnaire against DSM IV as a tool to diagnose major depressive disorder in Indian patients. *Journal of Postgraduate Medicine, 53*, 102–107.

Lasalvia, A., et al. (2015) Should the label 'schizophrenia' be abandoned? *Schizophrenia Research, 162*, 276–284.

Levin, T. (2006). Schizophrenia should be renamed to help educate the public. *The International Journal of Social Psychiatry, 52*, 324–331.

Lin, K. M. (1981). Traditional Chinese medical beliefs and their relevance for mental illness and psychiatry. In A. Kleinman, T. Y. Lin (Eds.), *Normal and abnormal behavior in Chinese Culture. Culture, illness, and healing* (vol. 2). Springer.

Malla, A., Joober, R., & Garcia, A. (2015). "Mental illness is like any other medical illness": A critical examination of the statement and its impact on patient care and society. *Journal of Psychiatry and Neuroscience, 40*(3), 147–150.

Boeschoten, M. A. et al. (2018). Development and evaluation of the Dutch clinician-administered PTSD scale for DSM-5 (CAPS-5). *European Journal of Psychotraumatology, 9*(1), 1546085.

Maruta, T., Matsumoto, C. (2017). Stigma and the renaming of schizophrenia. In W. Gaebel, W. Rössler, & N. Sartorius (Eds.), *The Stigma of Mental Illness – End of the Story?* (pp. 571–579). Springer.

Murray, R. M. (2006). Schizophrenia term use 'invalid'. *BBC News*, 9 October. Available at http://news.bbc.co.uk/2/hi/health/6033013.stm

Sanderson, K., & Andrews, G. (2022). Prevalence and severity of mental health-related disability and relationship to diagnosis. *Psychiatric Services, 53*(1), 80–86.

Sartorius, N. et al. (2014). Name change for schizophrenia. *Schizophrenia Bulletin, 40*(2), 255–258.

Schäffner, C. (1998). Skopos theory. In M. Baker, & G. Saldanha (Eds.), *Routledge encyclopedia of translation studies* (Vol. 17, pp. 235–238).

The Diagnostic and Statistical Manual of Mental Disorders (5th ed.) (2013) American Psychiatric Association.

Þórðarson, Ó. et al. (2020). Icelandic translation and reliability data on the DSM-5 version of the schedule for affective disorders and schizophrenia for school-aged children—present and lifetime version. *Nordic Journal of Psychiatry, 74*(6), 423–428.

Williams, J. (2013). *Theories of translation*. Springer.

Contents

1 **Introduction** 1
   1.1 Mental Health Worldwide 1
   1.2 Variations in the Expression of Mental Disorders 3
   1.3 Translating and Cross-Culturally Adapting Mental Health
        Scales: A Pressing Need 4
   1.4 Cultural Adaptation in the Translation of Mental Health Scales 7
        1.4.1 Content Equivalence 9
        1.4.2 Semantic Equivalence 9
        1.4.3 Technical Equivalence 10
        1.4.4 Criterion Equivalence 10
        1.4.5 Conceptual Equivalence 11
   1.5 Cultural Adaptation in Mental Health Translation as One Means
        to Reduce Stigmatization of Mental Illness 12
   1.6 Summary and Goal of This Book 14
   References 15

2 **Understanding Varying Mental Health Needs of People
from Diverse Cultural Backgrounds** 21
   References 25

3 **Cultural Relevance of Mental Health Scales** 27
   References 30

4 **Cultural Comprehensibility of Mental Health Scales** 33
   References 35

5 **Cultural Acceptability of Mental Health Scales** 37
   References 39

Appendix A: Translation of Mental Disorder Terms 41

Chapter 1
Introduction

Abstract This chapter begins with a brief review of the literature on global mental health. Variations in how mental health disorders are expressed are then reviewed, followed by a proposal of the necessity of the translation and cross-cultural adaptation of mental health scales. Subsequently, cultural adaptation in the context of health translation is discussed based on relevant literature. Through the review, proposal and discussion above, this study aimed to explore cultural adaptation in the translation of mental health scales as one means to reduce stigmatization of mental disorders and attend to the mental health needs of individuals with mental illness.

Keywords Mental health · Mental health materials · Translation · Cultural adaptation · Mental health needs · Destigmatization

1.1 Mental Health Worldwide

Population mental health is integral to population health (Susser & Patel, 2014), and there could be "no health without mental health" (Prince et al., 2007). Mental health is defined as "a state of well-being in which every individual realizes his or her own potential, can cope with the normal stresses of life, can work productively and fruitfully, and is able to make a contribution to her or his community" (World Health Organization, 2007). Such a state is, however, disrupted in at least one out of three people over their lifetime (Ginn & Horder, 2012; Steel et al., 2014). According to Mental Health Foundation (2015), 25% of adults and 10% of children are likely to suffer from mental illness every year. Mental illness has, therefore, become a growing public health concern globally (Mental Health Foundation, 2016), significantly impacting the life of millions of people and profoundly impacting the community and economy.

Global mental health, by definition, examines factors impacting health across national boundaries, promotes health equity within and among countries, addresses prevention and clinical care, and values mutual exchange of knowledge in partnerships among countries of different income levels (Koplan et al., 2009). One main objective of global mental health is to ascertain and meet the most glaring unsatisfied needs for mental health care in low- and medium-income countries (Collins et al., 2011; Horton, 2007; Lancet Global Mental Health Group, 2007; Menezes, 2014; Patel & Prince, 2010; Pike et al., 2013). Various other goals are also widely shared in the global mental health domain (Becker & Kleinman, 2013; Menezes, 2014; Pike et al., 2013), including "promoting social inclusion and civil rights of people with mental illness, combating stigma and discrimination, involving service users in shaping the care they receive and building regional and local capacity for mental health research" (Susser & Patel, 2014).

Regarded as one of the most common causes of disability, mental health disorders can impair the quality of life (Whiteford et al., 2015). Individuals with severe mental health disorders represent a socially vulnerable and excluded group (Funk et al., 2010). Their lives are more likely to be subject to poverty, discrimination, human rights violation and increased morbidity and mortality rates (Susser & Patel, 2014). Mental disorders are considered a major driver of the growing overall morbidity and mortality worldwide (Alonso et al., 2013; Prince et al., 2007). The socially disadvantaged groups of individuals with mental disorders tend to have less access to environments that stimulate social, emotional and cognitive development in early life, and these early disadvantages are associated with a range of worse mental health and social outcomes across their life course (Susser & Patel, 2014). However, individuals living with mental illness are largely neglected globally (Saxena et al., 2007).

It has been estimated that mental disorders may cost the global economy $16 trillion from 2011 to 2030 through lost labor and capital output (Jones et al., 2014). The average annual mental health burden for each of these twenty years may be equivalent to 1% of the 2012 global GDP (World Bank, 2023). From the broadest perspective, mental disorders are detrimental to "human capital" as the most valuable resource of modern societies and "human development" as the benchmark of progress because mental health is fundamental to both (Sen and Anand, 1990; Heckman, 2006; Jenkins et al., 2008; Sen, 1999).

In the context of the widely perceived negative impacts of mental health disorders on individual lives and society, the worldwide magnitude of mental disorders has been underscored by studies on their global burden (Lopez & Murray, 1998). However, despite the considerable worldwide burden and the associated adverse human, economic and social impacts, priority has not been given to the treatment and care of individuals with mental illness by policy makers and funders across the world (Bloom et al., 2011; Saxena et al., 2007) and by health professionals and providers worldwide. One underlying overriding cause is the lack of high quality translated materials related to mental disorders worldwide. Such translated materials can help fill the language gap that prevails in the mental health domain (Black, 2018), especially in the context that the growing perception of core symptoms of common mental disorders worldwide has greatly driven campaigns for addressing mental disorders in developing countries (Patel & Prince, 2010; World Health Organization (WHO), 2008).

1.2 Variations in the Expression of Mental Disorders

As is shown by large-scale epidemiological studies, mental disorders are prevalent in diverse societies and cultures (Flaherty et al., 1988). However, different global prevalence rates of major mental health disorders imply that there are variations in how these disorders are expressed (Flaherty et al., 1988; Draguns & Tanaka-Matsumi, 2003). These variations may partly be explained by the fact that people living in diverse social contexts experience and communicate emotional distress in different ways (Ballenger et al., 2001). As such, psychiatric disorders can be seen as cultural conventions, which mainly define appropriate forms and expressions of suffering (Kirmayer, 2002), resulting in largely variable manifestations, diverse presentations and unique illness categories across cultural settings (Desjarlais et al., 1995; Kirmayer, 2007). For example, Kirmayer (2002) has identified several different forms of mental illness specific to particular cultural settings that are expressed by means of idioms of distress.

Investigating mental health disorders in different cultures is controversial and can best be explained by two positions embedded in cross-cultural psychiatry: the universalistic position versus the relativistic position (Smit et al., 2006). The former holds that emotions result from neurophysiologic processes in the limbic system and are thus biological phenomena, and that there is a limited repertoire of universal emotional experiences (Panksepp, 1998). Advocated in biomedicine, this position highlights categorizing and labeling syndromes (Kleinman & Good, 1985). By contrast, the relativist position argues that emotional expression is socially constructed and thus specific to a given historical, societal and cultural system (Lutz, 1985). Held by ethnographic and anthropological studies, this position asserts that tools developed in one cultural setting may fail to capture the idiosyncratic ways that emotional distress is expressed in other cultural settings because the context within which people from other cultures live and experience the world may be ignored (Kleinman & Good, 1985).

Both positions have been criticized for their limitations. The universalistic position runs the risk of being imperialistic because it ignores cultural differences and insists on using concepts developed in a Western context as a blueprint for perceiving other cultures (Kleinman & Good, 1985). The relativistic position risks concretizing dissimilarities by ignoring the impacts of acculturation and cultural assimilation (Swartz, 1998), therefore revealing little about similarities (Kirmayer, 2001).

The relativistic position and the universalistic position align respectively with the *emic* and *etic* approaches, two traditional methods of observation adopted in cross-cultural research (Flaherty et al., 1988). These orientations are concerned with the origin of concepts in question (Draguns & Tanaka-Matsumi, 2003; Kinzie & Manson, 1987). As "an insider's view of culture," the emic approach, comparable to the relativistic position, aims at the description of the language and customs of the culture at a specific time by using "culturally defined, within-group independent and dependent (outcome) variables" to gain a granular understanding of concepts relevant to one cultural setting but possibly irrelevant to other cultural settings (Flaherty et al., 1988, p. 257). This approach can enable us to give a fine-grained description of behaviors within a particular culture at a given time, allowing for descriptively comparing particular phenomena between two cultures and theories to explain observed phenomena. In contrast, within the paradigm of the etic approach, comparable to the universalistic position, the concept of a behavior and techniques for measuring this behavior in one culture is applied to another culture, shedding little light on cultural disparities in the purpose and meaning of behavior (Flaherty et al., 1988). As a result, signs and symptoms of a prevalent disorder (i.e., depression) specific to a particular culture will be overlooked if diagnostic criteria established in a specific Western culture is applied to a non-Western cultural context (Kleinman, 1977). In brief, the emic approach focuses on the meaning that a specific cultural group attaches to a particular notion while the etic approach focuses on the description of phenomena that is independent of meaning (Kinzie & Manson, 1987).

In the final analysis, the nature of emic and etic approaches could largely be revealed by Murphy's (1969) claim that culture enters psychiatric inquiry in two ways: as a distortion and as an object of research. Specifically, the emic approach is adopted when one aims to compare the symptoms of commonly occurring syndromes, such as depression, cross-culturally; on the other hand, the etic approach is used when one seeks to identify the impact of acculturation on depressive symptoms across two particular cultures, and the objective of this approach is to minimize the distortion by culture to make cross-cultural comparisons meaningful (Flaherty et al., 1988).

Attempts have been made to integrate the relativistic and universalistic positions through combining the emic and etic approaches (Smit et al., 2006), with concepts and descriptions that are derived from anthropological studies (an emic orientation) being incorporated into measuring scales, an etic orientation (Draguns & Tanaka-Matsumi, 2003). Such integration finds its full expression in the process in which cultural equivalence is established through the cross-cultural adaptation of psychiatric research instruments (Smit et al., 2006).

In the context of a growing number of populations who could benefit from mental health materials written in their native language, it is necessary to determine an approach to language translation that prioritizes the world view of the target readers (Black, 2018). Such an approach is most likely to identify the variations in how mental disorders are expressed in the target language and cultural settings.

1.3 Translating and Cross-Culturally Adapting Mental Health Scales: A Pressing Need

Translation is essentially a multilingual and multicultural endeavor that can provide far-reaching implications for the growth and development of the mental health domain worldwide (Black, 2018). Culture can play a substantial role in variations in behaviour, and measurement of behavior in a cross-cultural context calls for the use of adapted instruments (Herdman et al., 1997). The global population (cultural) diversity entails a pressing need for cross-culturally validated measures or scales (Sousa & Rojjanasrirat, 2011), which can be used to ascertain the varying mental health needs of diverse populations from multicultural societies. This need necessitates the translation and cross-cultural adaptation of mental health scales. "Translation, adaptation and validation of an instrument or scale for cross-cultural research is time-consuming and requires careful planning and adoption of rigorous methodological approaches to derive a reliable and valid measure of the concept of interest in the target population." (Sousa & Rojjanasrirat, 2011) Mental health materials thus translated, adapted and validated are most likely to identify the variations in how mental health disorders are expressed in diverse language and cultural settings and therefore capture the varying health needs of multicultural populations across national boundaries and within multicultural communities. To facilitate comparability and deliver appropriate interventions, the best way to identify and assess mental disorders is likely to be an integration of adapting Western instruments (van Ommeren et al., 1999), exploring additional symptoms and expressions that would not be captured through an adaptation-only approach (Kohrt & Hruschka, 2010), and investigating far-reaching influences, including function impairment (Bolton & Tang, 2002).

When reviewing the literature on and proposing guidelines for cross-cultural adaptation of health-related quality of life measures, Guillemin et al., (1993, p. 1417) observe that "With a few exceptions, all the measures so far developed are in the English language and are intended for use in English-speaking countries." This is also true for other health-related materials, including various instruments like mental health scales. It is, therefore, necessary to have materials available in languages other than English for comprehensive and accurate cross-cultural research, assessment, and education (Johnson & Cameron, 2001; Miranda et al., 2002) in non-English-speaking countries and among a growing number of immigrants in English-speaking communities. Such necessity confirms the settings for cross-cultural adaptation of scales identified by Guillemin et al. (1993). The degree of adaptation depends on similarities and disparities between the languages and cultures of the populations concerned (Brislin et al., 1973). Immigrants recently settled in a host culture may have a low level of acculturation and thus need a measure that is cross-culturally adapted to their native language and culture. For example, immigrants living in America or Australia may encounter specific problems in communicating their needs in English with regard to health-related issues, and they may also assess their health status and perceive health materials of various types based on their language and cultural origin and the degree of being assimilated into the host language and culture. Besides, a scale to be administered in a country other than that where it has been developed may necessitate cross-cultural adaptation since different cultural beliefs have been imprinted in the mind of the people concerned, who are accustomed to referring to their native culture when assessing their health conditions and understanding health materials.

A huge range of English health-related measures have been developed and validated to administer various health-related assessment, screening, interventions, and education. "There is nonetheless a need for measures specifically designed to be used in non-English-speaking countries and also among immigrant populations, since cultural groups vary in disease expression and in their use of various health care systems." (Guillemin et al., 1993, p. 1417). To meet this need, two approaches can be adopted: developing new tools and using tools already developed in another language. Developing new scales is time-consuming (Shan et al., 2023), with the bulk of the effort made to conceptualize the scale and select and reduce its items (Guillemin et al., 1993). When previously developed measures are transposed through simple translation from their source cultural settings to target cultural contexts, they are most unlikely to be successful due to language and cultural differences (Berkanovic, 1980) and to cultural variations in the perception of particular concepts and constructs and the ways that health issues are expressed (Kleinman et al., 1978). Success in this approach calls for a systematic toolkit that can entail the effective cross-cultural adaptation of original English measures.

Cross-cultural adaptation consists of two essential components: the translation of the measures under investigation and its adaptation. It requires "a combination of the literal translation of individual words and sentences from one language to another and an adaptation with regard to idiom, and to cultural context and lifestyle" (Guillemin et al., 1993, p. 1421). The quality of an adapted instrument is then subjected to assessment with regard to its sensibility, the essential elements of which include the designed purpose, comprehensibility, content and face validity, replicability and suitability of the scale studied (Feinstein, 1987).

The individuals' perceptions of the scales studied and the ways that health problems are expressed and health situations are assessed vary from culture to culture (Guillemin et al., 1993; Kleinman et al., 1978). As a result, translating and adapting previously developed instruments cross-culturally may most likely accommodate the varying needs of the populations studied in the target language and culture. This is particularly true for the cross-cultural translation and adaptation of already developed mental health scales, given the growing global prevalence and magnitude of mental health disorders and the resulting burdens on and negative outcomes for the individual and society, as reviewed in Sect. 1.1. Trans-culturally adapting and validating previously developed instruments can facilitate communicating research findings to international audiences who are likely to fund mental health service development (Kohrt et al., 2011). Besides, adapting standardized measures for depression and anxiety can be beneficial with regard to administering treatment approaches tailored to such disorders (WHO, 2008). Filling the written language gap in mental health through translation and adaptation not merely helps increase the availability of multi-language written materials, but also helps open educational opportunities that are conventionally delivered through psychoeducation, parenting, preparedness workshops or other oral means (Black, 2018). Additionally, culturally and linguistically appropriate written educational materials promise not only to offer essential information, but also to reduce stigma socially attached to mental health concerns and relevant help-seeking (Black, 2018). One of the objectives of this work is to use cross-cultural adaptation as a means to contribute to the worldwide mental health stigma reduction initiatives. Section 1.5 will deal with this topic by focusing on the stigma attached to mental disorders and the role of language (translation), or more

1.4 Cultural Adaptation in the Translation of Mental Health Scales

"Research in the area of translation methodology has been largely overlooked in the mental health field" (Black, 2018). It is essential to cross-culturally adapt health-related instruments to obtain valid responses (Banville et al., 2000). Cultural adaptation of research scales is designed to produce culturally equivalent research materials. Translated and adapted scales catering to the cultural beliefs of the target language are key to accurately and comprehensively assessing individuals' health status, delivering tailored interventions, and therefore facilitating culturally appropriate and relevant health care (Banville et al., 2000). As such, we can say that "translation is, at its core, a multicultural and multilingual endeavor with profound implications for the growth and development of the mental health field on a global scale" (Black, 2018, p. 9).

An adapted tool may be deemed culturally equivalent when all types of biases or social norms unique to the source culture have been eliminated (Van de Vijver & Poortinga, 1997). According to Van de Vijver and Poortinga (1997), three categories of biases are likely to influence cross-cultural research, including construct bias, method bias and item bias. Construct bias may occur when the concept under discussion is substantially different cross-culturally. Method bias may occur when the methods adopted to investigate a construct are unfamiliar or inappropriate in the target culture. Item bias may occur when a particular item fails to fit the description of a concept under discussion in the target culture. Cultural adaptation is an effective approach to getting rid of these biases.

Cultural adaptation aims to achieve cultural equivalence, which consists of five major mutually-exclusive dimensions: content equivalence, semantic equivalence, technical equivalence, criterion equivalence, and conceptual equivalence (Flaherty et al., 1988, p. 258).

> *Content equivalence.* The concept of each item of the instrument is relevant to the phenomena of each culture being studied.
> *Semantic equivalence.* The meaning of each item is the same in each culture after translation into the language and idiom (written or oral) of each culture.
> *Technical equivalence.* The method of assessment (e.g., pencil and paper, interview) is comparable in each culture with respect to the data that it yields.
> *Criterion equivalence.* The interpretation of the measurement of the variable remains the same when compared with the norm for each culture studied.
> *Conceptual equivalence.* The instrument is measuring the same theoretical construct in each culture.

According to Flaherty et al. (1988), any item or measure may be cross-culturally equivalent on one or more of these five dimensions but not equivalent on other dimensions. For example, semantically equivalent instruments may not necessarily be conceptually equivalent ones. Figure 1.1 (Flaherty et al., 1988, p. 258) below can vividly illustrate these five dimensions of cultural equivalence.

As illustrated in Fig. 1.1, the 45° line represents a "culture-free" instrument, one that is equivalent on all five dimensions across culture A and culture B. Such cultural freedom or universality of measures is not a rule but an exception. In reality, instruments are culture-bound, as shown by the two 90° lines pointing to culture A and culture B in Fig. 1.1. The actual adaptation of scales across cultures, in effect, yields an oscillating line around the 45° line rather than a straight line at 45° for each tool adapted for study. The objective of this taxonomy is to facilitate designing a measure that is cross-culturally equivalent in all five dimensions. In what follows, these five dimensions of equivalence will be described in detail in the light of Flaherty et al. (1988), if not specified otherwise.

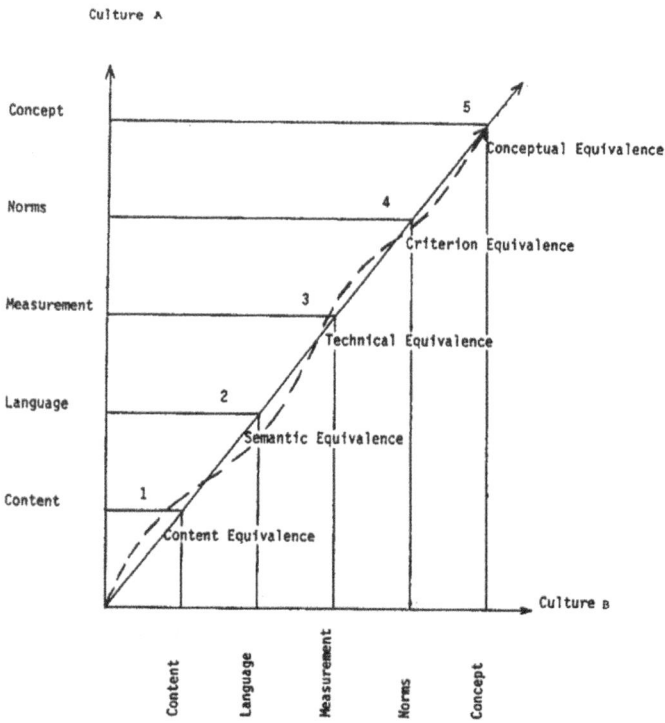

Fig. 1.1 Taxonomy of issues in designing instruments for cross-cultural validation in psychiatric research

1.4 Cultural Adaptation in the Translation of Mental Health Scales

1.4.1 Content Equivalence

For cross-cultural research, each item of the scale needs to be examined with fine granularity to ascertain whether the phenomenon described is relevant to each culture or not. When content validity has been established in the source culture, the relevance of each item to the target culture needs to be reexamined by determining whether the item, or rather the phenomenon the item describes, actually occurs in the target culture and is recognized by the members of the target culture.

A content expert team comprising social scientists and psychiatrists from both source and target cultures assesses the content equivalence of each instrument item by rating it as relevant, irrelevant, or questionably relevant to each target culture under investigation. Items rated as irrelevant by one expert or questionably relevant by two or more experts need to be directly removed; items rated as questionably relevant by one expert need to be reconsidered for inclusion.

When any item is crossed out, the modified tool needs to be scrutinized once more to determine internal consistency and reliability. To this end, standardized alpha coefficients are usually measured, with an alpha coefficient greater than 0.60 showing that a given instrument is acceptable. When many items are removed from a measure, its internal consistency may be so diminished that it could not be used in cross-cultural studies. If the variable assessed by the tool is essential to the research, new items need to be added to achieve content equivalence and restore internal consistency. Sometimes, we would modify some items by finding equivalent content areas in the source and target cultures on an item-by-item basis to yield two different scales that are equivalent in content. Modifications of tools by adding items for one culture produce tailor-made scales relevant to each culture, though not directly comparable any longer (Brislin, 1970).

1.4.2 Semantic Equivalence

Semantic equivalence is achieved when the meaning of each item remains unchanged after being translated into the language of each culture. It is particularly challenging to achieve semantic equivalence in cross-cultural studies. The usual practice in cross-cultural research is that a scale developed for use in one (source) culture and language is translated into another (target) language and culture. However, it is incorrect to assume that the translated scale would naturally be reliable and valid in the target culture.

Back-translation proposed by Brislin (1970) is generally acknowledged as the key to achieving semantic equivalence. A measure is forward-translated from a source language to a target language by one or more bilingual persons before being back-translated from the target language to the source language by another bilingual person or team. And then, a team of bilingual experts scrutinizes these two versions by rating each item on a 3-point Likert scale, with 3, 2, and 1 indicating "exactly the same meaning in both versions," "almost the same meaning in both versions," and "different meaning in each version."

Items rated as "different meaning in each version" by all raters need to be removed; items receiving a mix of ratings of "exactly the same meaning in both versions" and "almost the same meaning in both versions" need to be reconsidered. In many cases, rewording is not sufficient enough to allow an item or items to be included. Any reworded items need to be reexamined through back-translation. It is essential to reword rather than eliminate items if possible so as not to disturb the psychometric properties of the translated scale. Nevertheless, it is impossible to realize semantic equivalence on an item, particularly when translating either idioms or adjectives and terms that describe personal or emotional states.

Back-translation turns far more intricate when more than two cultures are being investigated and especially when merely an oral version of the language exists in a culture. Semantic equivalence calls for equivalence both to the source culture and to all target cultures under investigation.

1.4.3 Technical Equivalence

What really matters in technical equivalence is whether the data collection method impacts the research results differently in the source and target cultures. Some data collection methods regarded as natural in Western culture may be considered as uncomfortable or unfamiliar in some other cultures. For example, as pointed out by Vernon and Roberts (1981), the technical equivalence of a paper-and-pencil test is always compromised in cross-cultural research because this data collection method is unfamiliar to many countries in the third world. Similarly, private interviews of females by male interviewers are generally regarded as a taboo; the questionnaire formats of repeated questioning and probing prevalent in Western society may be deemed forcible in countries of the third world. A panel of experts familiar with the methods of data collection in both cultures needs to determine whether the data gathering method for each scale is consistent with the target culture.

1.4.4 Criterion Equivalence

In cross-cultural studies, criterion equivalence is designed to assess the capacity of the scale to evaluate the variables in both source and target cultures under investigation. Criterion equivalence is established when the interpretation of the results from the source tool and the target tool is the same in both cultures.

A scale developed in one culture is designed to differentiate individuals who are independently assessed as having a trait or diagnosis from those who are independently assessed as not having this trait or diagnosis. Ideally, the adapted tool has equally high levels of sensitivity or specificity when it is applied to the target culture.

If not, it is most likely that a different cutoff score is needed in the target culture although the adapted scale is able to distinguish individuals with the trait from those without it.

As with criterion equivalence, what is at issue is not whether particular phenomena or symptoms occur, but whether the diagnostic criteria actually assess the same phenomena in both cultures.

1.4.5 Conceptual Equivalence

Conceptually equivalent scales assess the same basic construct (concept) in different cultures. "Conceptual equivalence refers to the validity of the concept explored and the events experienced by people in the target culture, since items might be equivalent in semantic meaning but not conceptually equivalent" (Guillemin et al., 1993, p. 1423). For example, "Physical therapist" may be translated perfectly from English into Chinese semantically, but have a different conceptual meaning in the Chinese culture. Vernon and Roberts (1981, p. 1240) claim that a direct measurement of conceptual equivalence is usually impossible in psychiatry, and other less direct techniques are needed, including "examining the correlations among the items on the questionnaire in the study population and analyzing the relationship of responses to other variables in each study population."

The method usually adopted to determine conceptual equivalence is to examine the relationship between constructs as measured by the scale and to compare this relationship with their known relationship (Cronbach & Meehl, 1955). For example, if stressful life events are found to be positively correlated with psychophysiological symptoms in both cultures under study and if there exists a cross-culturally valid method to measure these symptoms, the finding of significant correlations between stressful life events and such symptoms could establish the conceptual equivalence of the life events tool cross-culturally (Baratta et al., 1985).

Health-related concepts are conceptualized and operationalized differently in different languages and cultures, highlighting the significance of exploring conceptual equivalence in the translation and adaptation of instruments (Sidani et al., 2010). Conceptual equivalence means the "existence, relevance, and acceptability of the concept and its indicators across cultures": the meaning, perception, and indicators of the concept in the source culture are similar to those in the target culture (Sidani et al., 2010, p. 134). It is reflected through recognizing and perceiving the concept and relevant indicators in the source and target cultures (Johnson, 2006; Stewart and Napoles-Springer, 2000). It is necessary to determine conceptual equivalence to minimize the risk of imposing a concept prevailing in one culture upon another culture where it is unfamiliar or irrelevant and the risk of failing to identify relevant indicators specific a concept in another culture (Brislin et al., 1973). Underlying the cultural validity of measures designed to assess health-related concepts (Leplege & Verdier, 1995), conceptual equivalence needs to be examined before translating instruments from the source language and culture to the target language and culture.

Although there are recommendations and guidelines with regard to translating, adapting and cross-validating instruments using a comprehensive multi-step process, researchers fail to put them into practice (Sousa & Rojjanasrirat, 2011). This failure is most possibly attributable to unspecified, user-unfriendly methodologies presented in previous studies, making it challenging for researchers to utilize these methodological approaches (Sousa & Rojjanasrirat, 2011). This background of research warrants the examination of cultural adaptation in the translation of health scales using a specified, use-friendly, comprehensive approach, which we will present in the translation of various genres of mental health materials.

The objective of translation is to achieve equivalence between the scale in the source language and the scale in the target language (Sperber, 2004). To this end, the symmetrical translation is a better choice, compared with the asymmetrical translation. The symmetrical translation is the most recommended approach because it attaches great importance to faithfulness of meaning and colloquialness of expression in both the source and target languages rather than to literal translation (Jones & Kay, 1992). It is the only approach that facilitates comparing responses from individuals of one culture with those of another (Jones & Kay, 1992; Jones et al., 2001) and determining the most relevant types of cross-cultural equivalence (semantic, conceptual, content, technical, and criterion) (Hilton & Skrutkowski, 2002). The process of translation, adaptation, and cross-cultural validation of a measure for use in other languages, cultures, and countries calls for well-considered planning and appropriate application of comprehensive, rigorous, and well-established methodologies (Chapman & Carter, 1979; Brislin, 1970, 1986; Jones, 1987; Jones & Kay, 1992; Guillemin et al., 1993; McDermott and Palchanes, 1994; Beaton et al., 2000, 2002; Jones et al., 2001; Sperber, 2004; Shan et al., 2023).

1.5 Cultural Adaptation in Mental Health Translation as One Means to Reduce Stigmatization of Mental Illness

Individuals with mental illness are far more intensely stigmatized than those suffering from other medical conditions, which frequently gives rise to unfavorable social, political, economic and psychological consequences (Baumann, 2007; El-Badri & Mellsop, 2007; Marwaha & Johnson, 2005). People are less likely to relate to those with mental illness (Halter, 2008). Stigmatizing attitudes lead to discriminatory practices in daily settings, limiting private and public institution opportunities (Pingani et al., 2012). Afraid of stigmatization, people with mental illness are likely to disengage themselves from society, therefore worsening their clinical conditions and prognosis (Mojtabai, 2010; Vauth et al., 2007; Yap et al., 2010). Pervasive stigma and discrimination contributes, to some extent, to the imbalance between the global burden of disease caused by mental disorders and the attention paid to these conditions (Vigo et al., 2016). Stigma is reflected in discriminating social structures, policy and legislation, resulting in lower availability, accessibility and quality of services geared to mental health, compared with physical health (Giesecke et al., 2004). Fewer job opportunities and social exclusion or bullying are typical examples of stigmatization (Pingani et al., 2012).

From the perspective of conceptualization, stigmatization may entail intricate cognitive-behavioral interactions between individuals and social settings (Norman et al., 2010). Two leading theoretical explanatory conceptualizations can well elucidate the complex social construct of stigma: Corrigan et al. (2003) and Link and Phelan (2001). According to Corrigan et al. (2003), public stigma can be conceptualized as status loss and discrimination attributable to prejudices towards individuals with mental illness held by people around them. Link and Phelan (2001) conceptualize self-stigma as the reactions of those belonging to a stigmatized population when coming face to face with stigmatizing attitudes that they apply to themselves. These two conceptual constructs consist of three components: the cognitive component of stereotypes, the emotional component of prejudice and the behavioral component of discrimination. Stereotypes can be defined as negative beliefs, attributed to other for public stigma (e.g., being dangerous or incompetent) or to self for self-stigma (e.g., belief of being dangerous or incompetent); stereotypes lead to prejudice as their cognitive and emotional reaction (e.g., fear or anger for public stigma, and low self-esteem for self-stigma) and subsequently to the behavioral response of discrimination (e.g., avoidance or withholding employment and housing opportunities for public stigma, and failure to pursue work for self-stigma) (Corrigan & Watson, 2002). Studies have identified a direct link between these three dimensions and recovery from psychiatric disorders: low levels of knowledge, stigmatizing attitudes and discriminatory behaviors are correlated with social exclusion and lower rates of help-seeking and medication compliance, all of which hamper care and treatment and thus prevent recovery (Evans-Lacko et al., 2012; Rüsch et al., 2005; Thornicroft, 2008). As with public stigma, two more concepts need to be described: the concept of responsibility and the concept of dangerousness. Responsibility is based on the attribution theory (Weiner, 1995): when individuals with mental disorders are regarded as being responsible for their disorders, the public may be angry with them and will not assist them; when individuals with mental disorders are deemed as a victim of mental disorders, feelings of pity and readiness to help will be evoked in the general public. The conceptualization of dangerousness asserts that people perceiving individuals with mental illness as dangerous will fear and thus avoid them (Edwards & Endler, 1989).

Studies have been conducted to diminish stigma attached to mental illness. In addition to a wide range of public health campaigns launched to reduce stigma attached to mental disorders, such as the Changing Mind Campaign by The Royal College of Psychiatrists in the UK (Crisp, 2000), the advocacy of the review of language used about people with mental disorders needs to be noticed and enhanced. For example, a review of the language used about people living with dementia has been advocated for inclusion, stigma reduction and the increase of education and awareness as the way to reduce stigma (Bartlett, 2014). The power of language has also been highlighted by Alzheimer's Australia (2009) in their Dementia Friendly Language Position Paper 4:

> Language is a powerful tool. The words we use can strongly influence how others treat or view people with dementia. For example referring to people with dementia as 'sufferers' or as 'victims' implies that they are helpless. This not only strips people of their dignity and self esteem, it reinforces inaccurate stereotypes and heightens the fear and stigma surrounding dementia.

Inspired by such activism, we propose that the tool of language be harnessed to combat mental illness-related stigma. In this respect, the power of language can never be overemphasized, as we will illustrate in the following chapters of this book.

Language is a powerful tool (Cayton, 2006; Sabat, 2001). Words reflect thoughts and feelings, displaying respect or disrespect (Swaffer, 2014). As advocated by Swaffer (2014), the words that we use not merely considerably impact how others perceive or treat individuals living with dementia, but also, perhaps more importantly, affect how people with dementia view themselves and interact with others, which may adversely influence their abilities to be empowered. Language can "promote and empower, enable and increase self-esteem, and encourage one's ability to self-help, or it can demean, devalue, disrespect and offend those we refer to" (Swaffer, 2014, p. 711). Thus informed, we propose that the language used about individuals with mental disorders should be "normal, inclusive, jargon-free, non-elitist, clear, straight-forward, non-judgmental," and centering on "the person not the disease or social care system, or language trends that come and go" (Swaffer, 2014, p. 711). As argued by Hughes et al. (2006), "Language creates the particularly human kind of rapport, of being together, that we are in a conversation together." Accordingly, it is imperative and pressing to adopt "inclusive, non-offensive language that supports the whole person positively, rather than negative demeaning language that stigmatizes and separates us" (Swaffer, 2014, p. 711).

Cultural stigma attached to mental illness (Gary, 2005), the lack of culturally specific instruments and the resulting risk of misdiagnosis (Johnson & Cameron, 2001) and language (Garcia & Duckett, 2009) have been listed as barriers to seeking mental health services and care. Among them, language has been identified as "the most common barrier in any health care setting" and "a risk factor with adverse outcomes" (Aboul-Enein & Ahmed, 2006, p. 168). To attend effectively to the mental health needs of individuals with mental illness and to reduce stigmatization of mental disorders, we need to translate mental health scales previously developed in English into other languages and pay close attention to cross-cultural adaptation in the translation process.

1.6 Summary and Goal of This Book

Our book investigates the necessity and effectiveness of cultural adaptation in the translation of mental health scales. In what follows, we will present the principles of culturally effective adaptation in the translation of mental health scales before dealing with different genres of mental health materials and the effective implementation of cultural adaptation in the translation of these genres.

While methodologies for translating, adapting and validating measures for use in cross-cultural health care studies have been well established (Brislin, 1970, 1986; Chapman & Carter, 1979; Guillemin et al., 1993; Jones, 1987; Jones & Kay, 1992; Jones et al., 2001; Wild et al., 2005), variations in the use of these methodological approaches are constantly prevalent in the literature on health care. As a result, there is a lack of apparent consensus among researchers on how to use or combine these approaches, a great variation in the essential qualifications translators need to have, and a scarcity of detailed information on the forward-translation, back-translation, validation, modification and refinement of scales (Sousa & Rojjanasrirat, 2011). This background of research warrants further examination of cross-cultural translation and adaptation of health assessment tools to meet the varying health needs of individuals from diverse language and cultural settings and thereby deliver quality care targeted at mental health disorders across the world, and to add to the literature.

References

Aboul-Enein, F. H., & Ahmed, F. (2006). How language barriers impact patient care: A commentary. *Journal of Cultural Diversity, 13*(3), 168–169.

Alonso, J., Chatterji, S., & He, Y. (2013). *The burdens of mental disorders: Global perspectives from the WHO world mental health surveys*. Cambridge University Press.

Alzheimer's Australia. (2009). *Dementia friendly language: Position paper 4*. http://www.fightdementia.org.au/dementia-friendly-language.aspx

Ballenger, J. C., Davidson, J. R., Lecrubier, Y., Nutt, D. J., Kirmayer, L. J., Lepine, J. P., et al. (2001). Consensus statement on transcultural issues in depression and anxiety from the international consensus group on depression and anxiety. *Journal of Clinical Psychiatry, 62*(13), 47–55.

Banville, D., Desrosiers, P., & Genet-Volet, Y. (2000). Translating questionnaires and inventories using a cross-cultural translation technique. *Journal of Teaching in Physical Education, 19*, 374–387.

Baratta, S., Colorio, C., & Zimmerman-Tansella, C. (1985). Inter-rater reliability of the Italian version of the Paykel scale of stressful life events. *Journal of Affective Disorders, 8*, 279–282.

Bartlett, R. (2014). The emergent modes of dementia activism. *Ageing and Society, 34*, 623–644.

Baumann, A. (2007). Stigmatization, social distance and exclusion because of mental illness: The individual with mental illness as a 'stranger.' *International Review of Psychiatry, 19*(2), 131–135.

Beaton, D. E., Bombardier, C., Guillemin, F., & Ferraz, M. B. (2002). *Recommendations for the cross-cultural adaptation of health status measures*. http://www.dash.iwh.on.ca/assets/images/pdfs/xculture2002.pdf. Accessed 1 Oct 2009

Beaton, D. E., Bombardier, C., Guillemin, F., & Ferraz, M. B. (2000). Guidelines for the process of cross-cultural adaptation of self-report measures. *Spine, 25*(24), 3186–3191.

Becker, A. E., & Kleinman, A. (2013). Mental health and the global agenda. *New England Journal of Medicine, 369*, 1380–1381.

Berkanovic, E. (1980). The effect of inadequate language translation on Hispanics' responses to health surveys. *American Journal of Public Health, 70*, 1273–1276.

Black, A. K. (2018). *Language translation for mental health materials: A comparison of current back-translation and skopostheorie-based methods*. All Theses and Dissertations.

Bloom, D. E., Cafiero, E. T., Jané-Llopis, E., et al. (2011). *The global economic burden of noncommunicable diseases*. Geneva.

Bolton, P., & Tang, A. (2002). An alternative approach to cross-cultural function assessment. *Social Psychiatry and Psychiatric Epidemiology, 37*(11), 537–543.

Brislin, R. W., Lonner, W. J., & Thorndike, R. M. (1973). Questionnaire wording and translation. In *Cross-cultural research methods* (pp. 32–58). Wiley.

Brislin, R. W. (1970). Back-translation for cross-cultural research. *Journal of Cross-Cultural Psychology, 1*, 185–216.

Brislin, R. W. (1986). The wording and translation of research instruments. In W. J. Lonner & J. W. Berry (Eds.), *Field methods in cross-cultural research* (pp. 137–164). Sage Publications.

Cayton, C. (2006). From childhood to childhood? Autonomy and dependence through the ages. In J. Hughes, S. Louw, & S. Sabat (Eds.), *Dementia: Mind, meaning, and the person e-Kindle*. Oxford University Press, Inc.

Chapman, D. W., & Carter, J. F. (1979). Translation procedures for the cross cultural use of measurement instruments. *Educational Evaluation and Policy Analysis, 1*(3), 71–76.

Collins, P. Y., Patel, V., Joestl, S. S., et al. (2011). Grand challenges in global mental health. *Nature, 475*, 27–30.

Corrigan, P. W., Thompson, V., Lambert, D., Sangster, Y., & Campbell, J. N. J. (2003). Perceptions of discrimination among persons with serious mental illness. *Psychiatric Services, 54*(8), 1105–1110.

Corrigan, P. W., & Watson, A. C. (2002). Understanding the impact of stigma on people with mental illness. *World Psychiatry, 1*(1), 16–20.

Crisp, A. (2000). Changing minds: Every family in the land. An update on the College's campaign. *Psychiatric Bulletin, 24*, 267–268.

Cronbach, L. J., & Meehl, P. E. (1955). Construct validity in psychological tests. *Psychometrika, 52*, 297–334.

Desjarlais, R., Eisenberg, L., Good, B., & Kleinman, A. (1995). *World mental health: Problems and priorities in low-income countries*. Oxford University Press.

Draguns, J. G., & Tanaka-Matsumi, J. (2003). Assessment of psychopathology across and within cultures: Issues and findings. *Behaviour Research and Therapy, 41*(7), 755–776.

Edwards, J. M., & Endler, N. S. (1989). Appraisal of stressful situations. *Personality and Individual Difference, 10*(1), 7–10.

El-Badri, S., & Mellsop, G. (2007). Stigma and quality of life as experienced by people with mental illness. *Australasian Psychiatry, 15*, 195–200.

Evans-Lacko, S., Brohan, E., Mojtabai, R., & Thornicroft, G. (2012). Association between public views of mental illness and self-stigma among individuals with mental illness in 14 European countries. *Psychological Medicine, 42*(8), 1741.

Feinstein, A. R. (1987). The theory and evaluation of sensibility. In A. R. Feinstein (Ed.), *Clinimetrics* (pp. 141–166). Yale University Press.

Flaherty, J. A., Gaviria, F. M., Pathak, D., Mitchell, T., Wintrob, R., Richman, J. A., et al. (1988). Developing instruments for cross-cultural psychiatric research. *Journal of Nervous Mental and Disorders, 176*(5), 257–263.

Funk, M., Drew, N., Freeman, M., et al. (2010) *Mental health and development: Targeting people with mental health conditions as a vulnerable group*. World Health Organization.

Gary, F. A. (2005). stigma: A barrier to mental health care among ethnic minorities.*Issues in Mental Health Nursing, 26*, 979–999. Retrieved from http://web.b.ebscohost.com.erl.lib.byu.edu/ehost/pdfviewer/pdfviewer?sid=db0c2d88-2cd5-4bd4-9e6f-428729ea33eb@sessionmgr115&vid=1&hid=122

Garcia, C. M., & Duckett, L. J. (2009). No te entiendo y tú no me entiendes: Language barriers among immigrant Latino adolescents seeking health care. *Journal of Cultural Diversity, 16*(3), 120–126.

Giesecke, T., Gracely, R. H., Grant, M. A. B., Nachemson, A., Petzke, F., Williams, D. A., et al. (2004). Evidence of augmented central pain processing in idiopathic chronic low back pain. *Arthritis and Rheumatism, 50*(2), 613–623.

References

Ginn, S., & Horder, J. (2012). "One in four" with a mental health problem: The anatomy of a statistic. *BMJ, 344*, e1302.

Guillemin, F., Bombardier, C., & Beaton, D. (1993). Cross-cultural Adaptation of health-related quality of life measure: Literature review and proposed guidelines. *Journal of Clinical Epidemiology, 46*(12), 1417–1432.

Halter, M. (2008). Perceived characteristics of psychiatric nurses: Stigma by association. *Archives of Psychiatric Nursing, 22*(1), 20–26.

Heckman, J. J. (2006). Skill formation and the economics of investing in disadvantaged children. *Science, 312*, 1900–1902.

Herdman, M., Fox-Rushby, J., & Badia, X. (1997). "Equivalence" and the translation and adaptation of health-related quality of life questionnaires. *Quality of Life Research, 6*, 237–247.

Hilton, A., & Skrutkowski, M. (2002). Translating instruments into other languages: Development and testing processes. *Cancer Nursing, 25*(1), 1–7.

Horton, R. (2007). Launching a new movement for mental health. *Lancet, 370*, 806.

Hughes, J., Louw, S., & Sabat, S. (2006). Seeing the whole. In J. Hughes, S. Louw, S. Sabat, & e-Kindle (Eds.), *Dementia: Mind, meaning, and the person*. Oxford University Press, Inc.

Jenkins, R., Meltzer, H., Jones, P. B., et al. (2008). Mental capital and wellbeing: Making the most of ourselves in the 21st century. In *Mental health: Future challenges*. Government Office for Science.

Johnson, J. L., & Cameron, M. C. (2001). Barriers to providing effective mental health services to American Indians. *Mental Health Services Research, 3*(4), 215–223.

Johnson, T. P. (2006). Methods and frameworks for cross cultural measurement. *Medical Care, 44*, S17–S20.

Jones, E. (1987). Translation of quantitative measures for use in cross-cultural research. *Nursing Research, 36*(5), 324–327.

Jones, E. G., & Kay, M. (1992). Instrumentation in cross-cultural research. *Nursing Research, 41*(3), 186–188.

Jones, P. S., Lee, J. W., Phillips, L. R., Zhang, X. E., & Jaceldo, K. B. (2001). An adaptation of Brislin's translation model for cross-cultural research. *Nursing Research, 50*(5), 300–304.

Jones, S. P., Patel, V., Saxena, S., Radcliffe, N., Ali Al-Marri, S., & Darzi, A. (2014). How Google's 'ten Things We Know To Be True' could guide the development of mental health mobile apps. *Health Affairs (Millwood), 33*(9), 1603–1611.

Kinzie, J. D., & Manson, S. M. (1987). The use of self-rating scales in cross-cultural psychiatry. *Hospital and Community Psychiatry, 38*(2), 190–196.

Kirmayer, L. J. (2001). Cultural variations in the clinical presentation of depression and anxiety: Implications for diagnosis and treatment. *Journal of Clinical Psychiatry, 62*(13), 22–28.

Kirmayer, L. J. (2002). Psychopharmacology in a globalizing world: The use of antidepressants in Japan. *Transcultural Psychiatry, 39*(3), 295–322.

Kirmayer, L. J. (2007). Psychotherapy and the cultural concept of the person. *Transcultural Psychiatry, 44*(2), 232–257.

Kleinman, A. M. (1977). Depression, somatization and the "new cross-cultural psychiatry." *Social Science and Medicine, 11*, 3–10.

Kleinman, A., Eisenberg, L., & Good, B. (1978). Culture, illness and care: Clinical lessons from anthropologic and cross-cultural research. *Annals Internal Medicine, 88*, 251–258.

Kleinman, A. M., & Good, B. (1985). Introduction: Culture and depression. In A. Kleinman & B. Good (Eds.), *Culture and depression: Studies in the anthropology and cross-cultural psychiatry of affect and disorder* (pp. 1–33). University of California Press.

Kohrt, B. A., & Hruschka, D. J. (2010). Nepali concepts of psychological trauma: The role of idioms of distress, ethnopsychology and ethnophysiology in alleviating suffering and preventing stigma. *Culture, Medicine, and Psychiatry, 34*(2), 322–352.

Kohrt, B. A., Jordans, M., Tol, W., Luitel, N., Maharjan, S., & Upadhaya, N. (2011). Validation of cross-cultural child mental health and psychosocial research instruments: Adapting the

depression self-rating scale and child PTSD symptom scale in Nepal. *BMC Psychiatry, 11*, 127–143.
Koplan, J. P., Bond, T. C., Merson, M. H., et al. (2009). Towards a common definition of global health. *Lancet, 373*, 1993–1995.
Lancet Global Mental Health Group. (2007). Scaling up services for mental disorders: A call for action. *Lancet, 370*, 1241–1252.
Leplege, A., & Verdier, A. (1995). The adaptation of health status measures: Methodological aspects of the translation procedure. In S. Schumaker & R. Berzon (Eds.), *The international assessment of health-related quality of life: Theory, translation, measurement and analysis* (pp. 93–101). Rapid Communication.
Link, B., & Phelan, J. (2001). Conceptualizing stigma. *Annual Review of Sociology, 27*, 363–385.
Lopez, A. D., & Murray, C. C. (1998). The global burden of disease, 1990–2020. *Nature Medicine, 4*(11), 1241–1243.
Lutz, C. (1985). Depression and the translation of emotional worlds. In A. Kleinman & B. Good (Eds.), *Culture and depression: Studies in the anthropology and cross-cultural psychiatry of affect and disorder* (pp. 63–100). University of California Press.
Marwaha, S., & Johnson, S. (2005). Views and experiences of employment among people with psychosis: A qualitative descriptive study. *International Journal of Social Psychiatry, 51*, 302–316.
McDermott, M. A. N., & Palchanes, K. (1994). A literature review of the critical elements in translation theory. *Image: Journal of Nursing Scholarship, 26*(2), 113–117.
Menezes, P. (2014). Commentary: Perspective from LMIC. *International Journal of Epidemiology, 43*, 301–303.
Mental Health Foundation. (2015). *Fundamental facts about mental health 2015*. Mental Health Foundation.
Mental Health Foundation. (2016). *Fundamental facts about mental health 2016*. Mental Health Foundation.
Miranda, J., Lawson, W., & Escobar, J. (2002). Ethnic minorities. *Mental Health Services Research, 4*(4), 231–237.
Mojtabai, R. (2010). Mental illness stigma and willingness to seek mental health care in the European Union. *Social Psychiatry and Psychiatric Epidemiology, 45*(7), 705–712.
Murphy, H. B. M. (1969). Handling the cultural dimension in psychiatric research. *Social Psychiatry, 4*, 11–15.
Norman, R. M., Sorrentino, R. M., Gawronski, B., Szeto, A. C., Ye, Y., & Windell, D. (2010). Attitudes and physical distance to an individual with schizophrenia: The moderating effect of self-transcendent values. *Social Psychiatry and Psychiatric Epidemiology, 45*(7), 751–758.
Panksepp, J. (1998). *The foundations of human and animal emotions*. Oxford University Press.
Patel, V., & Prince, M. (2010). Global mental health: A new global health field comes of age. *JAMA: the Journal of the American Medical Association, 303*(19), 1976–1977.
Pike, K., Susser, E., & Galea, S. (2013). Towards a healthier 2020: Advancing mental health as a global health priority. *Public Health Reviews, 35*, 1157.
Pingani, L., Forghieri, M., Ferrari, S., Ben-Zeev, D., Artoni, P., Mazzi, F., Palmieri, G., Rigatelli, M., & Corrigan, P. W. (2012). Stigma and discrimination toward mental illness: Translation and validation of the Italian version of the attribution questionnaire-27 (AQ-27-I). *Social Psychiatry and Psychiatric Epidemiology, 47*, 993–999.
Prince, M., Patel, V., Saxena, S., et al. (2007). No health without mental health. *Lancet, 370*, 859–877.
Rüsch, N., Angermeyer, M., & Corrigan, P. (2005). The stigma of mental illness: Concepts, forms, and consequences. *Psychiatrische Praxis, 32*(5), 221–232.
Sabat, S. (2001). *The experience of Alzheimer's disease: Life through a tangled veil*. Blackwell.
Saxena, S., Thornicroft, G., Knapp, M., & Whiteford, H. (2007). Resources for mental health: Scarcity, inequity, and inefficiency. *Lancet, 370*(9590), 878–889.

References

Sen, A., & Anand, S. (1990). *The concept of human development. Background paper for the human development report 1990.* Human Development Report Office.

Sen, A. (1999). *Development as freedom.* Knopf.

Shan, Y., Ji, M., Dong, Z., Xing, Z., Wang, D., & Cao, X. (2023). The Chinese version of the patient education materials assessment tool for printable materials: Translation, adaptation, and validation study. *Journal of Medical Internet Research, 25*, e39808.

Sidani, S., Guruge, S., Miranda, J., Ford-Gilboe, M., & Varcoe, C. (2010). Cultural adaptation and translation of measures: An integrated method. *Research in Nursing and Health, 33*, 133–143.

Smit, J., van den Berg, C. E., Bekker, L.-G., Seedat, S., & Stein, D. J. (2006). Translation and cross-cultural adaptation of a mental health battery in an African setting. *African Health Sciences, 6*(4), 215–222.

Sousa, V. D., & Rojjanasrirat, W. (2011). Translation, adaptation and validation of instruments or scales for use in cross-cultural health care research: A clear and user-friendly guideline. *Journal of Evaluation in Clinical Practice, 17*, 268–274.

Sperber, A. D. (2004). Translation and validation of study instruments for cross-cultural research. *Gastroenterology, 126*(1), S124–S128.

Steel, Z., Marnane, C., Iranpour, C., et al. (2014). The global prevalence of common mental disorders: A systematic review and meta-analysis 1980–2013. *International Journal of Epidemiology, 43*(2), 476–493.

Stewart, A. L., & Napoles-Springer, A. (2000). Health-related quality of life assessments in diverse population groups in the United States. *Medical Care, 38*(9 Suppl.), II-102–124.

Susser, E., & Patel, V. (2014). Psychiatric epidemiology and global mental health: Joining forces. *International Journal of Epidemiology, 43*(2), 287–293.

Swaffer, K. (2014). Dementia: Stigma, language, and dementia-friendly. *Dementia, 13*(6), 709–716.

Swartz, L. (1998). *Culture and mental health: A southern Africa review.* Oxford University Press.

Thornicroft, G. (2008). Stigma and discrimination limit access to mental health care. *Epidemiologia e Psichiatria Sociale, 17*(01), 14–19.

Van de Vijver, F., & Poortinga, Y. H. (1997). Towards an integrated analysis of bias in cross-cultural assessment. *European Journal of Psychological Assessment, 13*(1), 10–14.

van Ommeren, M., Sharma, B., Thapa, S., Makaju, R., Prasain, D., Bhattarai, R., & et al. (1999). Preparing instruments for transcultural research: use of the translation monitoring form with Nepali-speaking Bhutanese refugees. *Transcultural Psychiatry, 36*(3), 285–301.

Vauth, R., Kleim, B., Wirtz, M., & Corrigan, P. (2007). Self-efficacy and empowerment as outcomes of self-stigmatizing and coping in schizophrenia. *Psychiatry Research, 150*, 71–80.

Vernon, S. W., & Roberts, R. E. (1981). Measuring nonspecific psychological distress and other dimensions of psychopathology: Further observations on the problem. *Archives of General Psychiatry, 38*, 1239–1247.

Vigo, D., Thornicroft, G., & Atun, R. (2016). Estimating the true global burden of mental illness. *The Lancet Psychiatry, 3*(2), 171–178.

Weiner, B. (1995). *Judgment of responsibility: A foundation for a theory of social conduct.* Guilford press.

Whiteford, H. A., Ferrari, A. J., Degenhardt, L., Feigin, V., & Vos, T. (2015). The global burden of mental, neurological and substance use disorders: An analysis from the Global Burden of Disease Study 2010. *PLoS ONE, 10*(2), e0116820.

Wild, D., Grove, A., Martin, M., Eremenco, S., McElroy, S., Verjee-Lorenz, A., & Erikson, P. (2005). Principles of good practice for the translation and cultural adaptation processs for patient-reported outcomes (PRO) measures: Report of the ISPOR task force for translation and cultural adaptation. *Value in Health, 8*(2), 94–104.

World Health Organization. (2007). *What is mental health?* http://www.who.int/features/qa/62/en/.

World Health Organization (WHO.(2008. *Mental health gap action programme(mhGAP): Scaling up care for mental, neurological and substance abuse disorders.* WHO.

World Bank. (2023). GDP (current US$) [Internet]. World Bank. http://data.worldbank.org/indicator/NY.GDP.MKTP.CD

Yap, M. B., Wright, A., & Jorm, A. F. (2010). The influence of stigma on young people's help-seeking intentions and beliefs about the helpfulness of various sources of help. *Social Psychiatry and Psychiatric Epidemiology, 46*(12), 1257–1265.

Open Access This chapter is licensed under the terms of the Creative Commons Attribution-NonCommercial-NoDerivatives 4.0 International License (http://creativecommons.org/licenses/by-nc-nd/4.0/), which permits any noncommercial use, sharing, distribution and reproduction in any medium or format, as long as you give appropriate credit to the original author(s) and the source, provide a link to the Creative Commons license and indicate if you modified the licensed material. You do not have permission under this license to share adapted material derived from this chapter or parts of it.

The images or other third party material in this chapter are included in the chapter's Creative Commons license, unless indicated otherwise in a credit line to the material. If material is not included in the chapter's Creative Commons license and your intended use is not permitted by statutory regulation or exceeds the permitted use, you will need to obtain permission directly from the copyright holder.

Chapter 2
Understanding Varying Mental Health Needs of People from Diverse Cultural Backgrounds

Abstract This chapter justifies the need to understand varying mental health needs of people from diverse cultural backgrounds. It is true and widely acknowledged that there are diverse languages and cultures across the world, with unique languages and cultures specific to particular countries. Immigrants bring their native languages, customs and cultures to the hosting countries, resulting in increased diversity of languages and cultures within the boundaries of these receiving countries. With the ever-changing ethnic and cultural composition of such communities, the mental health needs among their populations are changing and becoming increasingly diversified. In this context, researchers are being propelled by such diversities to make research findings more applicable to various sub-populations, and health professionals are being required to deliver culturally and linguistically responsive care in different settings.

Keywords Mental health needs · Diverse cultural backgrounds

It is true and widely acknowledged that there are diverse languages and cultures across the world, with unique languages and cultures specific to particular countries. Such diversity is further complicated by the ever-growing trend of immigration, which is a reality across the world. Immigrants bring their native languages, customs and cultures to the hosting countries (Sidani et al., 2010), resulting in increased diversity of languages and cultures within the boundaries of these receiving countries, including the United States and Australia. For example, the linguistic and cultural diversity within America is wide and constantly expanding (Black, 2018). With the ever-changing ethnic and cultural composition of American communities, the mental health needs among American populations are changing (Shrestha & Heisler, 2011) and becoming increasingly diversified. This is true for Australia and other developed countries, which have become ideal immigration destinations, leading to increased linguistic and cultural diversity and thereby diversified health needs of subgroups of populations within these societies. There is, therefore, a pressing need for relevant cross-cultural studies to handle numerous problems among these multinational and multicultural populations (Sousa & Rojjanasrirat, 2011). Development of mental health initiatives has been called for at national and international (e.g., UNICEF, 2014; WHO, 2013) levels to address cultural diversities and the needs of local populations. In this context, researchers are being propelled by such diversities to make research findings more applicable to various sub-populations, and health professionals are being required to deliver culturally and linguistically responsive care in different settings (Sidani et al., 2010). "If people do not identify with the materials, they will reject it. If people do not see themselves in the message, they will not listen. If people do not understand the message, they will not respond." (Watters, 2003).

Health care researchers engaging in cross-cultural studies need to gain access to reliable and cross-validated measures in other languages and cultures (Beaton et al., 2000; Sousa et al., 2005). Since administering quality care is based on accurate measurement and better understanding of the linguistic, cultural and ethnic backgrounds of individuals, cross-cultural research findings can provide physicians, nurses and other health care professionals with essential clinical implications with regard to how to deliver care to diverse populations. As measurement of people's health conditions is a core component of health care (Sidani et al., 2010), various assessment tools specific to the diversified languages and cultures of people living in different countries and within multicultural communities are required to capture the varying physical and mental health needs of individuals from various language and cultural backgrounds. In short, the global population diversity suggests a pressing need for cross-culturally validated research scales or tools to enable researchers and clinicians to access reliable and valid instruments that capture concepts of interest unique to their particular languages and cultures and thereby to carry out cross-cultural studies and administer quality patient care (Sousa & Rojjanasrirat, 2011).

Cultural beliefs and values can shape individuals' understanding of health, interpretation of changes of health conditions and perceived acceptability of health interventions (Givens et al., 2007; Killoran & Moyer, 2006). As a result, people' perspectives on health vary from culture to culture, and health-related concepts are conceptualized and operationalized differently across cultures, resulting in varying health needs among people from diverse cultural contexts. The perception and interpretation and the indicators of particular health concepts in one culture may not necessarily make any sense in another culture (Banville et al., 2000; Yam et al., 2005). Health instruments are developed based on specific beliefs and values reflecting the dominant culture (Sidani et al., 2010) where these tools are designed and intended to be used, which impacts individuals' ability to understand and respond to these measures (Warnecke et al., 1997). People are, therefore, most likely to respond to items on assessment tools from their own perspectives, which may not necessarily be congruent with the intent underlying the scales, undermining the validity or accurate interpretation of the responses (Sidani et al., 2010). A good case in point is the idiom of "feeling blue," which is semantically equivalent to "depression" in the culture prevalent in North American. This culturally-loaded expression is included in many instruments for academic and clinical purposes, including Center for Epidemiologic Studies-Depression Scale (Radloff, 1977). The color blue, however, symbolizes "joy" in some Latin American cultures (Streiner & Norman, 2008) and "vigor and vitality," "peace," "hope," "tranquility," etc., in Chinese culture. Responses of people from the latter cultural settings may be congruent with their understanding of the cultural connotation of the scale item involving "feel blue," but their responses would be misinterpreted by health professionals or researchers from North American cultures. Such misinterpretations are likely to incur inaccurate measurement of individuals' health status and health care needs, which potentially jeopardizes the appropriateness and safety of health interventions and health care services. As such, it is imperative to translate and adapt health-related instruments to secure valid responses (Banville et al., 2000) capturing people's perspectives on health that are specific to the target culture. Translated measures that are fully adapted to the language, beliefs and values of the target culture are the prerequisite for the accurate and comprehensive measurement of individuals' health conditions, the selection of appropriate interventions, and thereby the support of culturally appropriate, understandable and relevant health care.

"The lack of culturally appropriate mental health assessment instruments is a major barrier to screening and evaluating efficacy of interventions. Simple translation of questionnaires produces misleading and inaccurate conclusions." (Kaiser et al., 2013, p. 532) To be effective in assessing the physical and mental health of individuals from different language and cultural backgrounds, instruments must be translated and adapted to accurately measure their health status, avoiding limiting the meaningfulness of collected data (Sidani et al., 2010). In the context of language and cultural diversities across countries and the increased language and cultural diversities within some countries, like Australia and America, due to immigration, langue barriers and diverse cultural beliefs and values highlight the significance of achieving cultural equivalence in the process of translating and adapting health-related scales. The achievement of cultural equivalence in such a process not only entails the understanding of varying health needs of people from different cultures but also facilitates capturing their diverse health needs through instruments tailor-made to specific cultures.

To meet the diversified health needs of multicultural populations, merely translating previously developed assessment tools is far from sufficient. A growing literature shows that the "single forward and back-translation" technique has been proven inadequate in ensuring the quality of translation, potentially resulting in a poorly-translated version (Brislin et al., 1973; Hambleton, 2001). Cross-cultural adaptation needs to go hand-in-hand with translation to make translated scales specific to the multiple health needs of people from multiple cultural settings. Adaptation is oriented towards producing an equivalent measure adapted to the target culture, which is a prerequisite for the investigation of cross-cultural differences (Guillemin et al., 1993). The complex, challenging translation and adaptation task calls for a combination of approaches (Hambleton, 2001). Only when the quality of translation and adaptation has been ensured and the corresponding process involved has been reported, is it possible that comparisons are made across studies and datasets, conclusions are drawn on the constructs assessed, or statements are made about culture differences (van Widenfelt et al., 2005), for the benefit of understanding and meeting the varying health needs of people from multiple cultural backgrounds. To the best of our knowledge based on literature review, cross-cultural adaptation in the translation of mental health instruments has not yet attracted close attention from the international academic community. Hopefully, through our current research, this domain of study will receive adequate attention to help address diversified mental health needs and deliver tailored quality mental health care and services among different populations across national boundaries and within multicultural communities. To these ends, translated health-related materials must be relevant to the cultural beliefs and values of the target social settings and culturally comprehensible and acceptable to the target readers.

Presentations of mental disorders vary according to settings, particularly where somatic, emotional or psychological expressions are crucially important (Desjarlais et al., 1995). Recognition of mental disorders is further complicated by diverse expectations of normal or acceptable behavior (Desjarlais et al., 1995; Good et al., 2007). As a result, many important terms in mental health, including labels for affective states, are considerably challenging to translate directly, considering the lack of direct, available translations, the nuances of language evolution and the considerations of popular usage of particular terms (Barger et al., 2010). "Translation for mental health materials should be consistent with clients' multicultural background and context, and should not assume the target text audience's worldview to be identical or inferior to that of the source text audience." (Black, 2018, p. 8) As a result, strict translation of tools has been proven insufficient in multiple settings (Betancourt et al., 2009; Kohrt & Hruschka, 2010). To address such insufficiency, we propose that translated instruments should be adapted to the target culture to capture cultural understandings and constructs (Allden et al., 2009), thereby becoming culturally relevant, comprehensible and acceptable in the target social settings. The rationale for our proposal can be found in previous studies (Baorong, 2009; Jabir, 2006; Nord, 1997; Vermeer, 2000). Advocating functional approaches to translation theories, Nord (1997) asserts that different settings require different renderings of the source text. Vermeer (2000) and Baorong (2009) both uphold "skopostheorie" that takes "skopos" (purpose) as the fundamental principle underlying translation. In other words, what drives the approach to the translation of any text is none other than the intent underlying the text rather than full faithfulness to the original text in terms of the word-for-word structure or the extra-lingual communicative effect (Jabir, 2006). Applying functional translation approaches, or specifically skopostheorie, to translation in the domain of mental health, van Ommeren et al. (1999) proposes an approach to the cross-cultural translation of mental health scales developed in different cultural settings, which focuses on three dimensions of equivalence: the relevance, comprehensibility, and acceptability of items on the instrument. These dimensions will be presented in Chaps. 3, 4, and 5, respectively.

References

Allden, K., Jones, L., Weissbecker, I., Wessells, M., et al. (2009). Mental health and psychosocial support in crisis and conflict: Report of the mental health working group. *Prehospital Disaster Medicine, 24*(4), S217-227.

Banville, D., Desrosiers, P., & Genet-Volet, Y. (2000). Translating questionnaires and inventories using a cross-cultural translation technique. *Journal of Teaching in Physical Education, 19*, 374–387.

Baorong, W. (2009). Translating publicity texts in the light of the skopos theory. *Translation Journal, 13*(1), 47.

Barger, B., Nabi, R., & Hong, L. Y. (2010). Standard back-translation procedures may not capture proper emotion concepts: A case study of Chinese disgust terms. *Emotion, 10*(5), 703–711.

Beaton, D. E., Bombardier, C., Guillemin, F., & Ferraz, M. B. (2000). Guidelines for the process of cross-cultural adaptation of self-report measures. *Spine, 25*(24), 3186–3191.

Betancourt, T. S., Speelman, L., Onyango, G., & Bolton, P. (2009). A qualitative study of mental health problems among children displaced by war in Northern Uganda. *Transcultural Psychiatry, 46*(2), 238–256.

Black, A. K. (2018). *Language translation for mental health materials: A comparison of current back-translation and skopostheorie-based methods.* All Theses and Dissertations

Brislin, R. W., Lonner, W. J., & Thorndike, R. M. (1973). Questionnaire wording and translation. In *Cross-cultural research methods* (pp. 32–58). Wiley.

Desjarlais, R., Eisenberg, L., Good, B., & Kleinman, A. (1995). *World mental health: Problems and priorities in low-income countries.* Oxford University Press.

Givens, J. L., Houston, T. K., Van Voorhees, B. W., Ford, D. E., & Cooper, L. A. (2007). Ethnicity and preferences for depression treatment. *General Hospital Psychiatry, 29*, 182–191.

Good, B., Subandi, S., & Good, M.-J.D. (2007). The subject of mental illness: Psychosis, mad violence, and subjectivity in Indonesia. In J. Biehl, B. Good, & A. Kleinman (Eds.), *Subjectivity: Ethnographic investigations* (pp. 243–272). University of California Press.

Guillemin, F., Bombardier, C., & Beaton, D. (1993). Cross-cultural adaptation of health-related quality of life measure: Literature review and proposed guidelines. *Journal of Clinical Epidemiology, 46*(12), 1417–1432.

Hambleton, R. K. (2001). The next generation of the ITC Test translation and adaptation guidelines. *European Journal of Psychological Assessment, 17*, 164–172.

Jabir, J. K. (2006). Skopos theory: Basic principles and deficiencies. *Journal of the College of Arts: University of Basrah, 41*, 37–46.

Kaiser, B. N., Kohrt, B. A., Keys, H. M., Khoury, N. M., & Brewster, A.-R.T. (2013). Strategies for assessing mental health in Haiti: Local instrument development and transcultural translation. *Transcultural Psychiatry, 50*(4), 532–558.

Killoran, M. C., & Moyer, A. (2006). Surgical treatment preferences in Chinese American women with early-stage breast cancer. *Psycho-Oncology, 15*, 969–984.

Kohrt, B. A., & Hruschka, D. J. (2010). Nepali concepts of psychological trauma: The role of idioms of distress, ethnopsychology and ethnophysiology in alleviating suffering and preventing stigma. *Culture, Medicine, and Psychiatry, 34*(2), 322–352.

Nord, C. (1997). *Translating as a purposeful activity: Functionalist approaches explained.* Jerome Publishing.

Radloff, L. S. (1977). The CES-D scale: A self-report depression scale for research in the general population. *Applied Psychological Measurement, 1*, 385–401.

Shrestha, L. B., Heisler, E. J. (2011). *The changing demographic profile of the United States.* (Congressional Research Service Document RL32701). Retrieved from https://fas.org/sgp/crs/misc/RL32701.pdf

Sidani, S., Guruge, S., Miranda, J., Ford-Gilboe, M., & Varcoe, C. (2010). Cultural adaptation and translation of measures: An integrated method. *Research in Nursing and Health, 33*, 133–143.

Sousa, V. D., & Rojjanasrirat, W. (2011). Translation, adaptation and validation of instruments or scales for use in cross-cultural health care research: A clear and user-friendly guideline. *Journal of Evaluation in Clinical Practice, 17*, 268–274.

Sousa, V. D., Zauszniewski, J. A., Mendes, I. A., & Zanetti, M. L. (2005). Cross-cultural equivalence and psychometric properties of the Portuguese version of the depressive cognition scale. *Journal of Nursing Measurement, 13*(2), 87–99.

Streiner, D. L., & Norman, G. R. (2008). *Health measurement scales: A practical guide to their development and use* (4th ed.). Oxford University Press.

United Nations Children's Fund (UNICEF). (2014). *The state of the world's children 2015: Executive summary*. Available from http://data.unicef.org/

van Ommeren, M., Sharma, B., Thapa, S., Makaju, R., Prasain, D., et al. (1999). Preparing instruments for transcultural research: Use of the translation monitoring form with Nepali-speaking Bhutanese refugees. *Transcultural Psychiatry, 36*(3), 285–301.

van Widenfelt, B. M., Treffers, P. D. A., de Beurs, E., Siebelink, B. M., & Koudijs, E. (2005). Translation and cross-cultural adaptation of assessment instruments used in psychological research with children and families. *Clinical Child and Family Psychology Review, 8*(2), 135–147.

Vermeer, H. J. (2000). Skopos and commission in translational action. (A. Chesterman, Trans.). In L. Venuti (Ed.), *The translation studies reader* (pp. 221–233). Routledge (Original work published 1989).

Warnecke, R. B., Johnson, T. P., Chavez, N., Sudman, S., O'Rourke, D. P., Lacey, L., & Horm, J. (1997). Improving question wording in surveys of culturally diverse populations. *Annals of Epidemiology, 7*, 334–342.

Watters, E. K. (2003). Literacy for health: An interdisciplinary model. *Journal off Transcultural Nursing, 14*(1), 48–53.

World Health Organisation (WHO). (2013). *Mental health action plan 2013–2020*. WHO Press. http://www.who.int/mental_health

Yam, W. K. L., Chow, S. M. K., & Ronen, G. M. (2005). Chinese version of the parent-proxy health-related quality of measure for children with epilepsy: Translation, cross-cultural adaptation, and reliability studies. *Epilepsy and Behavior, 7*, 697–707.

Open Access This chapter is licensed under the terms of the Creative Commons Attribution-NonCommercial-NoDerivatives 4.0 International License (http://creativecommons.org/licenses/by-nc-nd/4.0/), which permits any noncommercial use, sharing, distribution and reproduction in any medium or format, as long as you give appropriate credit to the original author(s) and the source, provide a link to the Creative Commons license and indicate if you modified the licensed material. You do not have permission under this license to share adapted material derived from this chapter or parts of it.

The images or other third party material in this chapter are included in the chapter's Creative Commons license, unless indicated otherwise in a credit line to the material. If material is not included in the chapter's Creative Commons license and your intended use is not permitted by statutory regulation or exceeds the permitted use, you will need to obtain permission directly from the copyright holder.

Chapter 3
Cultural Relevance of Mental Health Scales

Abstract This chapter defines and exemplifies cultural relevance in relation to the translation of mental health scales. In addition to linguistic validity and psychometric validity, cultural is another highly influential factor that strongly impacts the achievement of an equivalent translation. Thus informed, we propose that mental health scales, cross-culturally translated and adapted ones in particular, must be relevant to the target culture, especially considering the fact that the global psychological knowledge is derived primarily from research on populations from North America and Western Europe, thereby representing merely 5% of the world's population and neglecting the remaining 95%. Specifically, the goal of cross-culturally translating and adapting previously developed mental health instruments is to make these tools culturally valid, or specifically relevant to systems of meaning, knowledge, and action for the target cultural group and local context. To this end, the development of cross-culturally adapted scales involves a process of modifying existing measures to ensure cultural relevance, technically termed cultural grounding, or evidence-based cultural adaptation.

Keywords Cultural relevance · Translation · Mental health scales

Culture is defined as systems of meaning, knowledge and action (Nastasi & Hitchcock, 2016). According to Nastasi et al. (2017, pp. 137–138), culture, when perceived as a system of meaning, facilitates individuals and communities organizing the multiple components of their world into a coherent whole in a process of co-construction via social interaction; culture, when considered as a system of knowledge, "sanctions normative behaviors and other socially acceptable ways of acting, so that the constructed 'meaningful' world is consolidated, reinforced, transmitted, and maintained over generations"; as a system of action, culture is dynamically constructed, that is, its members can negotiate new meanings by acting upon their world. Culture is, therefore, not merely a shared system of meaning, but an individual system for interpreting the world and guiding action and an interpersonal system to aid communication (Nastasi et al., 2017, p. 138). Since culture reflects a set of people's shared beliefs, values and behavioral expectations, the individual's interpretation of these shared systems may be impacted by their experiences in multiple settings with varying cultural meanings. It can be seen that culture is co-constructed by its members in given contexts.

In addition to linguistic validity and psychometric validity, cultural is another highly influential factor that strongly impacts the achievement of an equivalent translation (Kuliś et al., 2011). Therefore, cultural differences need to be considered in the process of translating instruments not only when different languages are spoken in multiple countries, but also when one language is spoken in more than one country or in various regions within a single country (Kuliś et al., 2011). Taking cultural differences into consideration, Nastasi et al. (2017) argue that the aim of cultural co-construction applied to school mental health programming is the development and planned adaptation of culturally-relevant interventions. Thus informed, we propose that mental health scales, cross-culturally translated and adapted ones in particular, must be relevant to the target culture, especially considering the fact that the global psychological knowledge is derived primarily from research on populations from North America and Western Europe, thereby representing merely 5% of the world's population and neglecting the remaining 95% (Arnett, 2008). Specifically, the goal of cross-culturally translating and adapting previously developed mental health instruments is to make these tools culturally valid, or specifically "relevant to systems of meaning, knowledge, and action for the target cultural group and local context" (Nastasi et al., 2017). To this end, the development of cross-culturally adapted scales involves a process of modifying existing measures to ensure cultural relevance, technically termed "cultural grounding," or "evidence-based cultural adaptation" (Barrera et al., 2013; Colby et al., 2013). Thus, cross-cultural adaptation needs to be informed by knowledge of target populations and contexts, and it is ideally achieved through a systematic data collection process that leads to evidence-based cultural grounding (Nastasi & Hitchcock, 2016).

Cultural relevance is closely associated with content equivalence. When showing content equivalence, an instrument item is relevant to local experiences (van Ommeren et al., 1999). When asking a question about phenomena that have nothing to do with the underlying construct, an instrument item is irrelevant to the target culture (Manson, 1997). Assessing cultural relevance entails comparing the content of the items on mental health-related scales with the popular beliefs about and indicators of the concept that are prevalent in the target culture (Sidani et al., 2010). Items whose content is consistent with the cultural beliefs and manifestations of the target societies are deemed culturally relevant (Sidani et al., 2010). The assessment of cultural relevance is designed to identify: (1) items on the source scales that are relevant to the target culture; (2) items on the source scales that need to be modified to make them more relevant to the target culture; and (3) manifestations that capture the concept prevalent in the target culture but are not embodied in any of the items on the source scale (Sidani et al., 2010). Based on such identifications, modifications need to be made as follows: (1) items or expressions in items that are irrelevant to the target culture need to be removed from the translated scale; (2) culturally appropriate or colloquial expressions of the same idea need to be used in the target scale; (3)

items that reflect indicators of the concept specific to the target culture need to be added to the translated scale; and (4) specific, culturally relevant indicators that are commonly manifested in the target culture but not captured by any item on the source scale need to added to the translated scale.

When the definitions and indicators of some concepts expressed in the items on the original scales cannot be captured in the target language and culture, these concepts or even the entire items involving these concepts need to be removed from the translated and adapted scales. For example, we removed the item "To what extent do you think it is likely that Personality Disorders are a category of mental illness" from the Mental Health Literacy Scale (O'Connor & Casey, 2015) when translating and adapting this measure from English into Chinese, considering that most Chinese people would not understand the Chinese translation of "Personality Disorders" into "人格障碍." This is because the concept of "Personality Disorders" is largely irrelevant to the Chinese culture and almost never talked about among Chinese populations. The decision of removal was made by a panel of researchers consisting of bilingual translators, bilingual mental health professionals and mental health content experts based on discussion and the bilingual mental health professionals' clinical experience and practice. Similarly, when translating and adapting the item "People with [mental illnesses] need to take better care of their grooming (bathe, clean teeth, use deodorant)" on Day's Mental Illness Stigma Scale (Day et al., 2007), we deleted "deodorant" from this item due to the fact that "deodorant" is irrelevant to the Chinese people's daily living experiences. Chinese populations never use "deodorant" after a bath or a shower, which is contrary to Western culture where it is commonly used. If translated into "除臭剂" and retained in the translated Chinese scale, this term is most likely to cause confusion among Chinese people and even stigmatize individuals with mental illness due to the possibly perceived association between odor and those suffering mental disorders. As the examples above indicate, removing items from and adding items to adapted scales entail carefully weighing the "trade-off" between making scales conceptually equivalent in the source and target languages and improving their cultural validity or relevance (Leplege & Verdier, 1995).

Some items on the source scales call for modifications to be more culturally relevant to the target social context. In this case, culturally appropriate or colloquial expressions of the same idea need to be used in the translated and adapted scale. A good case in point is the term "Agoraphobia" in the item "To what extent do you think it is likely that the diagnosis of Agoraphobia includes anxiety about situations where escape may be difficult or embarrassing" on the Mental Health Literacy Scale (O'Connor & Casey, 2015). "Agoraphobia," the fear of open or public places, is translated into "广场(或旷野)恐怖(症)," "恐旷症," or "公共场所恐惧症" in the dictionary, but not all these three translated versions are culturally appropriate from the perspective of the intended Chinese readers. We chose "广场恐惧症" as the final translation of "Agoraphobia" after consulting with several psychiatric professionals working in Qilu Hospital of Shandong University, China, who voted "广场恐惧症" as the most culturally appropriate or colloquial expression of the same idea as "Agoraphobia" in the original English item. Likewise, in cultural settings where some people in a particular ethnic group are not willing to acknowledge their condition of depression, "stressed" is a better wording in the adapted interventions (Conner & Grote, 2008). Different ethnic groups may have varying conceptualizations of mental disorders relative to the standard, established views of mental health professionals (Conner & Grote, 2008), which calls for linguistic modifications of certain terms or expressions in particular items on the translated and adapted scales to make them more culturally relevant.

To assess the cultural relevance of translated and adapted instruments, Sidani et al., (2010, p. 138) proposed the following questions: "Do you and people in your community believe and/or experience what this item reflects? How important is the idea or indicator reflected in this item in representing the concept as understood by you and people of your community? Is the content of the item offensive to people of your community? What words in your language can be used to express the same idea or indicator as in this item?" These questions can serve as specific indicators and yardsticks of cultural relevance in the translation and adaptation of mental health scales.

References

Arnett, J. J. (2008). The neglected 95%: Why American psychology needs to be less American. *American Psychologist, 63*, 602–614.

Barrera, M., Castro, F. G., Strycker, L. A., & Toobert, D. J. (2013). Cultural adaptations of behavioral health interventions: A progress report. *Journal of Consulting and Clinical Psychology, 81*(2), 703–711.

Colby, M., Hecht, M. L., Miller-Day, M., Krieger, J. L., Syvertsen, A. K., Graham, J. W., & Pettigrew, J. (2013). Adapting school-based substance use prevention curriculum through cultural grounding: A review and exemplar of adaptation processes for rural schools. *American Journal of Community Psychology, 51*, 190–205.

Conner, K. O., & Grote, N. K. (2008). Enhancing the cultural relevance of empirically-supported mental health interventions. *Families in Society: The Journal of Contemporary Human Services, 89*(4), 587–595.

Day, E. N., Edgren, K., & Eshleman, A. (2007). Measuring stigma toward mental illness: Development and application of the mental illness stigma scale. *Journal of Applied Social Psychology, 37*(10), 2191–2219.

Kuliś, D., Arnott, M., Greimel, E. R., Bottomley, A., & Koller, M. (2011). Trends in translation requests and arising issues regarding cultural adaptation. *Expert Review of Pharmacoeconomics and Outcomes Research, 11*(3), 307–314.

Leplege, A., & Verdier, A. (1995). The adaptation of health status measures: Methodological aspects of the translation procedure. In S. Schumaker & R. Berzon (Eds.), *The international assessment of health-related quality of life: Theory, translation, measurement and analysis* (pp. 93–101). Rapid Communication.

Manson, S. M. (1997). Cross-cultural and multi-ethnic assessment of trauma. In J. P. Wilson & T. M. Keane (Eds.), *Assessing psychological trauma and PTSD: A handbook for practitioners* (pp. 239–266). Guilford.

Nastasi, B. K., Arora, P. G., & Varjas, K. (2017). The meaning and importance of cultural construction for global development. *International Journal of School and Educational Psychology, 5*(3), 137–140.

Nastasi, B. K., & Hitchcock, J. (2016). *Mixed methods research and culture-specific interventions: Program design and evaluation*. Sage.

References

O'Connor, M., & Casey, L. (2015). The mental health literacy scale (MHLS): A new scale-based measure of mental health literacy. *Psychiatry Research, 229*, 511–516.

Sidani, S., Guruge, S., Miranda, J., Ford-Gilboe, M., & Varcoe, C. (2010). Cultural adaptation and translation of measures: An integrated method. *Research in Nursing and Health, 33*, 133–143.

van Ommeren, M., Sharma, B., Thapa, S., Makaju, R., Prasain, D., et al. (1999). Preparing instruments for transcultural research: Use of the translation monitoring form with Nepali-speaking Bhutanese refugees. *Transcultural Psychiatry, 36*(3), 285–301.

Open Access This chapter is licensed under the terms of the Creative Commons Attribution-NonCommercial-NoDerivatives 4.0 International License (http://creativecommons.org/licenses/by-nc-nd/4.0/), which permits any noncommercial use, sharing, distribution and reproduction in any medium or format, as long as you give appropriate credit to the original author(s) and the source, provide a link to the Creative Commons license and indicate if you modified the licensed material. You do not have permission under this license to share adapted material derived from this chapter or parts of it.

The images or other third party material in this chapter are included in the chapter's Creative Commons license, unless indicated otherwise in a credit line to the material. If material is not included in the chapter's Creative Commons license and your intended use is not permitted by statutory regulation or exceeds the permitted use, you will need to obtain permission directly from the copyright holder.

Chapter 4
Cultural Comprehensibility of Mental Health Scales

Abstract This chapter defines and exemplifies cultural comprehensibility in relation to the translation of mental health scales. Cultural beliefs and values shape individuals' understanding of health, interpretation of the changes of health status, and perception of the acceptability of health interventions. Therefore, language barriers and cultural beliefs impacts people's ability to understand and respond to these tools, limiting the meaningfulness of data collected. It is imperative to enhance the cultural comprehensibility of translated and adapted mental health scales.

Keywords Cultural comprehensibility · Translation · Mental health scales

Cultural beliefs and values shape individuals' understanding of health, interpretation of the changes of health status, and perception of the acceptability of health interventions (Givens et al., 2007; Killoran & Moyer, 2006). For instance, health measures are developed based on specific beliefs and values that represent those prevalent in the scientific community and the dominant culture. Therefore, language barriers and cultural beliefs impacts people's ability to understand and respond to these tools (Warnecke et al., 1997), limiting the meaningfulness of data collected. It is imperative to enhance the cultural comprehensibility of translated and adapted mental health scales.

Cultural comprehensibility is closely associated with semantic equivalence. When displaying semantic equivalence, an instrument item is comprehensible (van Ommeren et al., 1999). An incomprehensible translation, on the contrary, lacks semantic equivalence (Flaherty et al., 1988). Assessing comprehensibility entails determining the extent to which the content of the items on the translated and adapted scale can be clearly understood by target-language readers (Sidani et al., 2010). Therefore, we must pay close attention to well-considered planning before translation and to meticulous operation during translation. Before translation, we need to clarify the definition and indicators of the concept captured by selected instrument items to gain a better understanding of the meaning involved, while sharing target-language words or expressions that best capture the content and response options of these items (Sidani et al., 2010). During translation, we need to attach great importance to rendering the meaning of the items rather than to translating the items word for word, and to choosing simple, clear wording that can be easily understood by a target audience with lower educational attainment (i.e., Year 6) (Banville et al., 2000; Eremenco et al., 2005).

Because of cultural disparities, particular concepts that are obvious to one cultural community might be entirely incomprehensible and obscure to another. To facilitate comprehensibility, some researchers, like Brislin et al. (1973) and McGorry (2000), advocated "decentering," a strategy of rewording the source-language items in the simpler terms and sentence structures or examples to promote comprehension, which is referenced by much of the literature on translation currently cited in the domain of mental health (Brislin, 1980; Carlson, 1997; Cha et al., 2007). Rather than regarding the source text as static and unchangeable, decentering entails considering the source and target texts equal in importance and allows for modifications of the source text during translation to ensure equivalence between these two texts (Black, 2018). Take the translation and adaptation of "become romantically involved with someone" in the item "I would be less likely to become romantically involved with someone if I knew they were mentally ill" on the Prejudice towards People with Mental Scale (Kenny et al., 2018). We translated "become romantically involved with someone" into an easily understandable Chinese expression "谈恋爱" to help our target readers understand the translated item and thus the intended semantic meaning of the original item. In the same vein, "a close relationship" and "on an emotional roller coaster" in the item "A close relationship with someone with a mental illness would be like living on an emotional roller coaster" on Day's Mental Illness Stigma Scale (Day et al., 2007) were translated and adapted into the Chinese expressions of "谈恋爱" and "情绪可能会不太稳定, 会经历情绪上的大起大落" respectively to enhance cultural comprehensibility. Based on our expert panel discussion, we reworded the Chinese literal translations of "a close relationship" that is obvious to readers of the source (English) language but entirely obscure to readers of the target (Chinese) language, and of the metaphorical expression of "on an emotional roller coaster" that is likely to be misleading or puzzling among the intended Chinese populations. The reworded Chinese versions of "谈恋爱" and "情绪可能会不太稳定, 会经历情绪上的大起大落" are the most appropriate translated versions, not only retaining the original meaning of the concept in the source instrument (Leplege & Verdier, 1995), but also using idiomatic cultural expressions of the target language that are expressed in simple, easily-comprehensible wording (Sidani et al., 2010). In this way, semantic equivalence is established between the source and target items, ensuring the cultural comprehensibility of the adapted item among Chinese populations.

References

Banville, D., Desrosiers, P., & Genet-Volet, Y. (2000). Translating questionnaires and inventories using a cross-cultural translation technique. *Journal of Teaching in Physical Education, 19*, 374–387.

Black, A. K. (2018). *Language translation for mental health materials: A comparison of current back-translation and skopostheorie-based methods.* All Theses and Dissertations.

Brislin, R. W., Lonner, W. J., & Thorndike, R. M. (1973). Questionnaire wording and translation. In *Cross-cultural research methods* (pp. 32–58). Wiley.

Brislin, R. W. (1980). Cross-cultural research methods. In I. Altman, & A. Rapoport (Eds.), *Environment and culture.* Springer.

Carlson, E. D. (1997). A case study in translation methodology using the health-promotion lifestyle profile II. *Public Health Nursing, 17*(1), 61–70.

Cha, E. S., Kim, K. H., & Erlen, J. A. (2007). Translation of scales in cross-cultural research: Issues and techniques. *Journal of Advanced Nursing, 58*(4), 386–395.

Day, E. N., Edgren, K., & Eshleman, A. (2007). Measuring stigma toward mental illness: Development and application of the mental illness stigma scale. *Journal of Applied Social Psychology, 37*(10), 2191–2219.

Eremenco, S. L., Cella, D., & Arnold, B. (2005). A comprehensive method for the translation and cross-cultural validation of health status questionnaires. *Evaluation and the Health Professions, 28*, 212–232.

Flaherty, J. A., Gaviria, F. M., Pathak, D., Mitchell, T., Wintrob, R., Richman, J. A., et al. (1988). Developing instruments for cross-cultural psychiatric research. *Journal of Nervous Mental and Disorders, 176*(5), 257–263.

Givens, J. L., Houston, T. K., Van Voorhees, B. W., Ford, D. E., & Cooper, L. A. (2007). Ethnicity and preferences for depression treatment. *General Hospital Psychiatry, 29*, 182–191.

Kenny, A., Bizumic, B., & Griffiths, K. M. (2018). The Prejudice towards People with Mental Illness (PPMI) scale: Structure and validity. *BMC Psychiatry, 18*, 293.

Killoran, M. C., & Moyer, A. (2006). Surgical treatment preferences in Chinese American women with early-stage breast cancer. *Psycho-Oncology, 15*, 969–984.

Leplege, A., & Verdier, A. (1995). The adaptation of health statusmeasures: Methodological aspects of the translation procedure. In S. Schumaker & R. Berzon (Eds.), *The international assessment of health-related quality of life: Theory, translation, measurement and analysis* (pp. 93–101). Rapid Communication.

McGorry, S. (2000). Measurement in a cross-cultural environment: Survey translation issues. *Qualitative Market Research: An International Journal, 3*(2), 74–81.

Sidani, S., Guruge, S., Miranda, J., Ford-Gilboe, M., & Varcoe, C. (2010). Cultural adaptation and translation of measures: An integrated method. *Research in Nursing and Health, 33*, 133–143.

van Ommeren, M., Sharma, B., Thapa, S., Makaju, R., Prasain, D., et al. (1999). Preparing instruments for transcultural research: Use of the translation monitoring form with Nepali-speaking Bhutanese refugees. *Transcultural Psychiatry, 36*(3), 285–301.

Warnecke, R. B., Johnson, T. P., Chavez, N., Sudman, S., O'Rourke, D. P., Lacey, L., & Horm, J. (1997). Improving question wording in surveys of culturally diverse populations. *Annals of Epidemiology, 7*, 334–342.

Open Access This chapter is licensed under the terms of the Creative Commons Attribution-NonCommercial-NoDerivatives 4.0 International License (http://creativecommons.org/licenses/by-nc-nd/4.0/), which permits any noncommercial use, sharing, distribution and reproduction in any medium or format, as long as you give appropriate credit to the original author(s) and the source, provide a link to the Creative Commons license and indicate if you modified the licensed material. You do not have permission under this license to share adapted material derived from this chapter or parts of it.

The images or other third party material in this chapter are included in the chapter's Creative Commons license, unless indicated otherwise in a credit line to the material. If material is not included in the chapter's Creative Commons license and your intended use is not permitted by statutory regulation or exceeds the permitted use, you will need to obtain permission directly from the copyright holder.

Chapter 5
Cultural Acceptability of Mental Health Scales

Abstract This chapter defines and exemplifies cultural acceptability in relation to the translation of mental health scales. Cultural factors need to be appropriately dealt with in the translation of instruments developed in the source languages and cultures into the target languages and cultures. To solicit valid data, translated and adapted mental health scales must be culturally acceptable to the target readers. Cultural acceptability is closely associated with technical equivalence. When displaying semantic equivalence, which means that the method and impact of evaluation remain consistent, an instrument item is acceptable.

Keywords Cultural comprehensibility · Translation · Mental health scales

Cultural disparities must be considered not only when multiple languages are spoken in different countries, but also when one language is spoken in more than one country or in different regions within a country (Kuliś et al., 2011). As such, cultural factors need to be appropriately dealt with in the translation of instruments developed in the source languages and cultures into the target languages and cultures. To solicit valid data, translated and adapted mental health scales must be culturally acceptable to the target readers. Cultural acceptability is closely associated with technical equivalence. When displaying semantic equivalence, which means that "the method and impact of evaluation remain consistent," an instrument item is acceptable (van Ommeren et al., 1999, p. 534).

The cultural acceptability of translated mental health scales can be easily undermined by cultural-dependent issues. Such issues can be divided into two types: specific cultural issues and topical cultural issues. Specific cultural issues involve any specific concepts that may not be known to other cultures; topical cultural issues are related to questionnaire items that are associated with sensitive or offensive topics in particular cultures (Kuliś et al., 2011). These two categories of cultural issues need to be prioritized in the translation and adaptation of mental health scales to enhance cultural acceptability.

Concepts specific to certain cultures must be adapted to the target culture. This is because particular concepts that are obvious to one group of people may be completely obscure to another (Kuliś et al., 2011). Item 7 on the Psychiatric Scepticism Scale (Swami & Furnham, 2011) can serve as a good example of such a potentially obscure concept in an adapted Chinese scale. This item reads: "Psychiatry inappropriately excludes other approaches (e.g. alternative medicine) to mental distress." For western readers, like Australians or Americans, "alternative medicine" is clearly defined and stands in stark contrast to mainstream, evidence-based western medicine. When being forcefully translated literally into "替代医学," Chinese readers would be most likely to be confused in terms of what this translation drives at, for such a Chinese version does not make any sense in the context of Chinese language and culture due to the lack of such a concept or construct in Chinese language and cultural settings. Considering the unacceptability of this Chinese version to Chinese readers, we rendered "alternative medicine" into "非西医的各种传统医学" (various traditional medicines other than western medicine) and provided specific instances, "针灸" (acupuncture) and "草药" (herbal medicine), for this relatively abstract translation to enhance acceptability. A similar good case in point is "the clergy" in Choice E of Item B5a "Most people in treatment for depression are treated by which of the following?" on the 33-item Version of the Multiple-Choice Knowledge of Mental Illnesses Test (MC-KOMIT) (Compton et al., 2011). In western countries, like Australia and America, "the clergy" is a household name, but this concept is entirely new or strange to the Chinese culture. The forced, literal translation of "神职人员" would thus be unacceptable to Chinese readers who never engage in a relevant lived experience with a clergy. Considering this, we deleted this choice from the translated Chinese item. Choice C "Primary care physicians" in the same item could also be misleading to Chinese readers if being translated into "初级保健医生" literally or into "社区医生" using a foreignization translation approach. There is no "初级保健医生" or "社区医生" in mainland China, where people usually go to hospital to visit and consult a doctor when they are out of condition physically or mentally. Such a practice is different from that in Europe, America, and Hong Kong, where individuals first visit and consult their "primary care physician" before it is necessary to go to hospital with a referral from the latter. This is true for Choice B "Family therapist" in the same item. Since there is no "family therapist" in mainland China, the Chinese translation of "家庭治疗师" is, therefore, equally unacceptable to Chinese readers. Considering the unacceptability of the Chinese translation of these choices of Item B5a on MC-KOMIT (Compton et al., 2011), we deleted this item from the translated Chinese scale.

Sensitive or offensive topics or terms in particular cultures pose great obstacles to the translation of mental health scales. While sexuality can be a topic open to discussion in some western cultures, it is a taboo topic in the majority of eastern societies. Kalra et al. (2015) discussed the relationship between sexuality and mental health. Although we acknowledge that sexuality can positively contribute to mental health, we need to pay close attention to rewording when translating sex-related items on mental health scales. The solution to translating such items is to retain these problematic items but to thoroughly scrutinize each possible option of rewording through pilot tests among people (Kalra et al., 2015). The terms and constructions suggested by pilot-testing respondents can be relatively more acceptable to the target readers.

Each suggestion should be subjected to analysis by an expert panel consisting of bilingual translators, mental health professionals, content experts, and scale developers in terms of acceptability from the perspectives of the source and target cultures. In this way, the best rewording can prove to be the preferable solution to the problematic items and is finally confirmed by respondents through additional interviews.

References

Compton, M. T., Hankerson-Dyson, D., & Broussard, B. (2011). Development, item analysis, and initial reliability and validity of a multiple-choice knowledge of mental illnesses test for lay samples. *Psychiatry Research, 189*, 141–148.

Kalra, G., Ventriglio, A., & Bhugra, D. (2015). Sexuality and mental health: Issues and what next? *International Review of Psychiatry, 27*(5), 463–469.

Kuliś, D., Arnott, M., Greimel, E. R., Bottomley, A., & Koller, M. (2011). Trends in translation requests and arising issues regarding cultural adaptation. *Expert Review of Pharmacoeconomics and Outcomes Research, 11*(3), 307–314.

Swami, V., & Furnham, A. (2011). Preliminary examination of the psychometric properties of the psychiatric scepticism scale. *Scandinavian Journal of Psychology, 52*(4), 399–403.

van Ommeren, M., Sharma, B., Thapa, S., Makaju, R., Prasain, D., et al. (1999). Preparing instruments for transcultural research: Use of the translation monitoring form with Nepali-speaking Bhutanese refugees. *Transcultural Psychiatry, 36*(3), 285–301.

Open Access This chapter is licensed under the terms of the Creative Commons Attribution-NonCommercial-NoDerivatives 4.0 International License (http://creativecommons.org/licenses/by-nc-nd/4.0/), which permits any noncommercial use, sharing, distribution and reproduction in any medium or format, as long as you give appropriate credit to the original author(s) and the source, provide a link to the Creative Commons license and indicate if you modified the licensed material. You do not have permission under this license to share adapted material derived from this chapter or parts of it.

The images or other third party material in this chapter are included in the chapter's Creative Commons license, unless indicated otherwise in a credit line to the material. If material is not included in the chapter's Creative Commons license and your intended use is not permitted by statutory regulation or exceeds the permitted use, you will need to obtain permission directly from the copyright holder.

Appendix A
Translation of Mental Disorder Terms

42 Appendix A: Translation of Mental Disorder Terms

Source	English	Forward translation Chinese	Cultural adaptation translation	Backward translation English	Cultural adaptation
Day's mental illness stigma scale	There are effective medications for [mental illnesses] that allow people to return to normal and productive lives. (Treatability)	有治疗[精神疾病]的有效药物,可以让人们恢复正常和有成效的生活。(可治疗性)	有治疗[精神疾病]的有效药物,能让人们回到正常、充实的生活。(可治疗性)	There are effective medications for [mental illness] that can return people to normal, fulfilling lives. (Treatability)	Cultural comprehensibility
Day's mental illness stigma scale	I probably wouldn't know that someone has [a mental illness] unless I was told. (Visibility; reverse-scored)	除非有人告诉我,否则我可能不会知道某人患有[精神疾病]。(可见度；反向计分)	如果没有人告诉我,否则我可能看不出来[精神疾病患者。(可见性；反向得分)	If no one had told me otherwise, I might not have been able to recognise people with mental illness. (Visibility; reverse-scored)	Cultural comprehensibility
Day's mental illness stigma scale	People with [mental illnesses] tend to neglect their appearance. (Hygiene)	患有[精神疾病]的人往往忽视自己的外表。(卫生)	患有[精神疾病]的人往往不注意个人形象。(个人卫生)	People with [mental illness] tend not to take care of their personal appearance. (Personal hygiene)	Cultural comprehensibility
Day's mental illness stigma scale	It would be difficult to have a close meaningful relationship with someone with [a mental illness]. (Relationship Disruption)	很难与患有精神疾病]的人建立有意义的亲密关系。(关系中断)	和患有[精神疾病]的人建立相互关爱、相互关爱的亲密关系会很难。(人际关系受阻)	It can be difficult to have a loving, caring, intimate relationship with someone who has [mental illness]. (Interpersonal relationships are impeded)	Cultural relevance
Day's mental illness stigma scale	A close relationship with someone with [a mental illness] would be like living on an emotional roller coaster. (Relationship Disruption)	与患有[精神疾病]的人保持亲密关系就像生活在情绪的过山车上。(关系中断)	和患有[精神疾病]的人发展亲密关系可能会让人在情感上时而兴奋,时而低落。情绪变化很大,不太稳定。(人际关系受阻)	Developing a close relationship with someone who suffers from [mental illness] can be emotionally exciting at times and emotionally draining at others. Moods are highly variable and less stable. (Interpersonal relationships are impaired)	Cultural relevance

(continued)

Appendix A: Translation of Mental Disorder Terms

Source	English	Forward translation Chinese	Cultural adaptation translation	Backward translation English	Cultural adaptation
Day's mental illness stigma scale	There is little that can be done to control the symptoms of [mental illness]. (Treatability; reverse-scored)	几乎没有什么可以控制精神疾病的症状。(可治疗性:反向计分)	很难控制[精神疾病]的症状。(可治疗性;反向得分)	It is very difficult to manage symptoms [of mental illness]. (treatability; reverse scoring)	Cultural comprehensibility
Day's mental illness stigma scale	I think that a personal relationship with someone with [a mental illness] would be too demanding. (Relationship Disruption)	我认为与患有[精神疾病]的人建立私人关系要求太高。	我觉得很难跟患有精神疾病的人相处、发展人际关系。(人际关系受阻)	I find it hard to get along and develop relationships with people who have [mental illness]. (Interpersonal relationships are impeded)	Cultural comprehensibility
Day's mental illness stigma scale	People with [mental illnesses] ignore their hygiene, such as bathing and using deodorant. (Hygiene)	精神疾病患者会忽视自己的卫生,比如洗澡和使用除臭剂。(卫生)	[精神疾病]患者不注意个人卫生,比如不洗澡和身体除臭剂等。(个人卫生)	People with [mental illnesses] do not observe personal hygiene, such as not bathing and body deodorant. (Personal hygiene)	Cultural relevance
Day's mental illness stigma scale	I don't think that I can really relax and be myself when I'm around someone with [a mental illness]. (Anxiety)	我觉得当我看到有[精神疾病]的人在一起时,我无法放松下来做我自己。	当我和患有[精神疾病]的人在一起时,我无法完全放松下来,自在相处。(焦虑)	When I'm around people with [mental illness], I can't fully relax and be comfortable around them. (Anxiety)	Cultural relevance
Day's mental illness stigma scale	Psychiatrists and psychologists have the knowledge and skills needed to effectively treat [mental illnesses]. (Professional Efficacy)	精神科医生和心理学家拥有有效治疗[精神疾病]所需的知识和技能。(专业效率)	精神科医生和心理学专家有所需的知识和技能来有效地治疗[精神疾病]。(医术)	Psychiatrists and psychologists have the knowledge and skills needed to effectively treat [mental illness]. (Medical expertise)	Cultural relevance

(continued)

Appendix A: Translation of Mental Disorder Terms

(continued)

Source	English	Forward translation Chinese	Cultural adaptation translation	Backward translation English	Cultural adaptation
Mental health literacy scale	If someone became extremely nervous or anxious in one or more situations with other people (e.g., a party) or performance situations (e.g., presenting at a meeting) in which they were afraid of being evaluated by others and that they would act in a way that was humiliating or feel embarrassed, then to what extent do you think it is likely they have Social Phobia?	如果某人在一种或多种与他人相处的情境(如聚会)或表演情境(如在会议上发言)中变得极度紧张或焦虑,害怕被他人评价,害怕自己的行为会羞辱他人或您感到羞辱,那么您认为他在多大程度上可能患有社交恐惧症?	如果一个人出现以下行为,那么你认为他患有社交恐惧症的可能性有多大? 1. 个人在与他人交往的一个或多个场合(如聚会)变得极度紧张或焦虑(如会议发言),他们很担心其他人对他们的评论,或者他们的行为会羞辱他人或者他们自己会觉得很羞辱。 2. 公开场合(如会议发言),他们很担心其他人对他们的评论,或者他们的行为会羞辱他人或者他们自己会觉得很羞辱。	How likely do you think it is that a person has social phobia if they exhibit the following behaviors?1. A person becomes extremely nervous or anxious in one or more situations where they are interacting with others (e.g., parties)2. In public (e.g., speaking at a meeting), they are worried about what other people will say about them, or that their behavior will humiliate others or they themselves will feel embarrassed.	Cultural comprehensibility
Mental health literacy scale	To what extent do you think it is likely that *Dysthymia* is a disorder?	您认为心境恶劣是一种疾病的可能性有多大?	你认为持续性抑郁障碍可能是一种疾病吗?	Do you think persistent depressive disorder might be a disease?	Cultural comprehensibility
Mental health literacy scale	To what extent do you think it is likely that the diagnosis of *Agoraphobia* includes anxiety about situations where escape may be difficult or embarrassing?	您认为广场恐惧症的诊断在多大程度上包括对逃跑可能困难或羞害的情况的焦虑?	如果一个人因为担心脱身某个场所会很难或是会感到非常焦虑而觉得这个人多大可能患有广场焦虑症?	If a person becomes very anxious because they are worried that getting out of a place will be difficult or embarrassing, how likely do you think that person is to suffer from Square Anxiety Disorder?	Cultural comprehensibility

(continued)

Appendix A: Translation of Mental Disorder Terms

Source	English	Forward translation Chinese	Cultural adaptation translation	Backward translation English	Cultural adaptation
Mental health literacy scale	To what extent do you think it is likely that the diagnosis of Bipolar Disorder includes experiencing periods of elevated (i.e., high) and periods of depressed (i.e., low) mood?	您认为双相情感障碍的诊断在多大程度上可能经历情绪高涨(即高)和抑郁(即低)的时期?	你认为双相情感障碍的诊断是否可能包括人们经历情绪高涨(感觉非常兴奋)和情绪低落(感觉非常悲伤)的时期?	Do you think a diagnosis of bipolar disorder might include people experiencing periods of high mood (feeling very excited) and low mood (feeling very sad)?	Cultural comprehensibility
Mental health literacy scale	To what extent do you think it would be helpful for someone to improve their quality of sleep if they were having difficulties managing their emotions (e.g., becoming very anxious or depressed)?	如果某人在情绪管理方面遇到困难(如变得非常焦虑或抑郁),您认为提高其睡眠质量在多大程度上会有帮助?	如果一个人很难控制自己的情绪(比如变得非常焦虑或抑郁),你认为提高他们的睡眠质量会对他们有多大帮助?	If a person is having a hard time controlling their emotions (e.g. becoming very anxious or depressed), how much do you think improving the quality of their sleep would help them?	Cultural comprehensibility
Mental health literacy scale	To what extent do you think it would be helpful for someone to avoid all activities or situations that made them feel anxious if they were having difficulties managing their emotions?	如果一个人难以控制自己的情绪,您认为在多大程度上避免所有会让他感到焦虑的活动或情境会对他有帮助?	如果有人很难控制自己的情绪,你认为让他们完全避免所有感到焦虑的活动或场所,场合会对他们会有多大帮助?	If someone has a hard time controlling their emotions, how much do you think it would help them to completely avoid all activities or places and situations where they feel anxious?	Cultural comprehensibility
Mental health literacy scale	To what extent do you think it is likely that Cognitive Behaviour Therapy (CBT) is a therapy based on challenging negative thoughts and increasing helpful behaviours?	您认为认知行为疗法(CBT)在多大程度上可能是一种基于挑战消极思想和增加有益行为的疗法?	您认为认知行为疗法(CBT)是一种帮助人们改变消极想法并采取有助于病情好转的行为的治疗方法吗?	Do you think Cognitive Behavioral Therapy (CBT) is a treatment that helps people change negative thoughts and adopt behaviors that help them get better?	Cultural comprehensibility

(continued)

Source	English	Forward translation Chinese	Cultural adaptation translation	Backward translation English	Cultural adaptation
(continued)					
Mental health literacy scale	Mental health professionals are bound by confidentiality; however there are certain conditions under which this does not apply. To what extent do you think it is likely that the following is a condition that would allow a mental health professional to break confidentiality: If you are at immediate risk of harm to yourself or others.	心理健康专业人员受保密原则的约束,但是,在某些情况下,保密原则并不适用。你认为在以下情况上允许心理健康专业人员打破保密协议:如果你面临伤害自己或他人的直接风险。	心理健康专家有保密的义务,但也会有例外。你觉得在以下条件下,心理健康专家大可能不再为病人保密? 当你随时有伤害自己或他人的风险时。	Mental health professionals have a duty of confidentiality, but there can be exceptions. How likely do you think it is that a mental health professional will no longer maintain patient confidentiality under the following conditions? When you are at risk of harming yourself or others at any time.	Cultural comprehensibility
Mental health literacy scale	To what extent do you think it is likely that the following is a condition that would allow a mental health professional to break confidentiality: If your problem is not life-threatening and they want to assist others to better support you?	如果您的问题不危及生命而目的是帮助其他人更好地支持您,那么您认为在多大程度上心理健康专业人员打破保密协议?	当您的心理问题不会危及生命时,您觉得心理健康专家有多大可能会把您的心理问题告诉其他人,以便其他人给您更多的支持和帮助?	When your psychological problems are not life-threatening, how likely do you think it is that a mental health professional will tell others about your psychological problems so that others can give you more support and help?	Cultural comprehensibility
Mental health literacy scale	I am confident I have access to resources (e.g., GP, internet, friends) that I can use to seek information about mental illness.	我确信我可以利用各种资源(如全科医生、互联网、朋友)来寻求有关精神疾病的信息。	我可以充分使用各种资源来获取有关心理疾病的信息,如家庭医生、互联网、朋友。	I have full access to resources for information about mental illness, such as my family doctor, the Internet, and friends.	Cultural comprehensibility

(continued)

Appendix A: Translation of Mental Disorder Terms

Source	English	Forward translation Chinese	Cultural adaptation translation	Backward translation English	Cultural adaptation
Mental health literacy scale	People with a mental illness could snap out if it if they wanted.	患有精神疾病的人只要愿意，就能振作起来。	只要患有精神疾病的人愿意，就可以自己好起来。	People with mental illness can get better on their own if they want to.	Cultural comprehensibility
Mental health literacy scale	Seeing a mental health professional means you are not strong enough to manage your own difficulties.	去看心理健康专家意味着您还没有足够的力量来应对自己的困难。	去看心理健康专家意味着你不够坚强，无法应对自身的各种困难。	Going to a mental health professional means you are not strong enough to cope with your own difficulties.	Cultural comprehensibility
Mental health literacy scale	How willing would you be to move next door to someone with a mental illness?	你愿多愿意搬到精神病患者的隔壁？	你愿意和患有精神疾病的人做邻居吗?	Would you want to be a neighbor to someone with a mental illness?	Cultural comprehensibility
Mental health literacy scale	How willing would you be to spend an evening socialising with someone with a mental illness?	您愿意花一个晚上与患有精神疾病的人进行社交活动吗？	你会愿意和患有精神疾病的人一起出去活动吗，如吃饭、聊天、逛商场？	Would you be willing to go out with someone with a mental illness for an evening activity, such as dinner, conversation, shopping at the mall?	Cultural relevance
Mental health literacy scale	How willing would you be to vote for a politician if you knew they had suffered a mental illness?	Not applicable in China			Cultural acceptability
The prejudice towards people with mental scale	I usually find people with mental illness to be consistent in their behaviour.	我通常发现有精神疾病的人的行为是一致的。	我发现精神病患者的行为不太会反常。	I find that people with mental illnesses are less likely to behave erratically.	Cultural comprehensibility
Knowledge of depression MCQ test	1. Which of the following statements about clinical depression is FALSE?	1. 关于临床抑郁症，以下哪种说法是错误的?	1. 下列关于重度抑郁症的陈述哪一项是错误的?	1. Which of the following statements about major depressive disorder is false?	Cultural comprehensibility

(continued)

Source	English	Forward translation Chinese	Cultural adaptation translation	Backward translation English	Cultural adaptation
Knowledge of depression MCQ test	a. One in 1000 b. One in 50 c. One in 3 d. One in 1	a. 1000 分之一 b. 50 分之一 c. 3 分之一 d. 1 分之一	a. 0.1% b. 2% c. 30% D. 100%		Cultural acceptability
Knowledge of depression MCQ test	a. Depression does not begin in adolescence.	a. 抑郁症并不是开始于青春期。	a. 菁少年 (10-19岁)不会发病。	Adolescents (10–19 years old) do not develop the disease.	Cultural comprehensibility
Knowledge of depression MCQ test	c. Depression appears for the first time in middle-aged people.	c. 抑郁症往往初次显现于中年人阶段。	c. 抑郁症在中年开始发病。	Depression begins to develop in midlife.	Cultural comprehensibility
Knowledge of depression MCQ test	7. Which of the following behavior is associated with poor outcome?	7. 哪一种行为可能导致不良后果?	8. 以下哪种行为会使抑郁症的治疗效果不好?	8. which of the following behaviors would make treatment for depression less effective?	Cultural comprehensibility
Knowledge of depression MCQ test	a. Prolonged severe grief over loved ones	a. 对亲人的长期严重悲伤	a. 长时间沉浸在失去亲人的痛苦中	A long time to wallow in the pain of losing a loved one	Cultural acceptability
Knowledge of depression MCQ test	a. Changes in sleep patterns	a. 睡眠模式的改变	a. 睡觉不规律	Irregular sleep	Cultural comprehensibility
Knowledge of depression MCQ test	c. Loss of energy	c. 能量损失	没有力气	Lacking in strength	Cultural comprehensibility
Knowledge of depression MCQ test	a. Negative thinking that can lead to self-defeating or suicidal behavior	a. 消极思维可能导致自毁或自杀行为	A. 可能会导致自轻自贱或自杀行为的消极想法	Negative thinking that can lead to self-deprecating or suicidal behavior	Cultural acceptability
Knowledge of depression MCQ test	a. Poor motivation b. Normal energy c. Guilty thoughts d. Fatigue	a. 动力不足 b. 精力正常 c. 有负罪感 d. 疲倦	a. 积极性不高 b. 精力正常 c. 有负罪感 d. 疲倦	a. low motivation b. normal energy c. feelings of guilt d. fatigue	Cultural acceptability

(continued)

Appendix A: Translation of Mental Disorder Terms

(continued)

Source	English	Forward translation Chinese	Cultural adaptation translation	Backward translation English	Cultural adaptation
Knowledge of depression MCQ test	a. Medication b. Talk therapy. c. Light therapy (photo-therapy). d. Kiekie therapy		Kiekie therapy is not available in China.		Cultural relevance
Knowledge of depression MCQ test	b. Sleep disturbances	睡眠障碍	b. 睡不好	Unable sleep well	Cultural comprehensibility
Knowledge of depression MCQ test	c. Sexual side-effects (e.g. problems with sexual desire or orgasm)	性副作用(如性欲或性高潮问题)	c. 对性生活产生不好的影响(影响性欲和性高潮)	Bad effect on sex life (affects libido and orgasm)	Cultural acceptability
Knowledge of depression MCQ test	20. Which is FALSE about the effectiveness of antidepressant medications?	20. 关于抗抑郁药物的有效性, 哪一项是错误的?	20. 关于抗抑郁药的功效, 以下哪一项是错误的?	Which of the following is false regarding the efficacy of antidepressants?	Cultural comprehensibility
Knowledge of depression MCQ test	b. Moderate symptom improvement may take few weeks to be achieved in those who will respond.	对于那些有反应的人来说, 症状可能的时间中等程度的改善。	b. 对于那些有反应的人来说, 症状可能需要几周时间才会有一些改善。	For those who do respond, it may take a few weeks for the symptoms to show some improvement.	Cultural comprehensibility
Knowledge of depression MCQ test	a. Both individual and group talk therapy provides an opportunity to express and discuss thoughts and feelings with the therapist.	个人和团体该话疗法都提供了一个与治疗师表达和讨论想法与感受的机会。	个人该话治疗和患者组成的团体该话治疗都提供了与治疗师表达和讨论想法和感受的机会。	Both individual talk therapy and group talk therapy with patients provide opportunities to express and discuss thoughts and feelings with the therapist.	Cultural relevance

(continued)

(continued)

Source	English	Forward translation Chinese	Cultural adaptation translation	Backward translation English	Cultural adaptation
33-item version of the multiple-choice knowledge of mental illnesses test (MC-KOMIT)	C. Legal restraining orders	C. 法律限制令	C. 法院下达的禁令	Court-ordered injunctions	Cultural relevance
33-item version of the multiple-choice knowledge of mental illnesses test (MC-KOMIT)	E. Support groups	E. 支持小组	E. 互助小组	Mutual aid groups	Cultural relevance
33-item version of the multiple-choice knowledge of mental illnesses test (MC-KOMIT)	A. Assisted living facility	A. 辅助生活设施	A. 提供专业辅助服务的老年人群聚生活社区	Cluster living communities for the elderly with specialized assistive services	Cultural relevance
33-item version of the multiple-choice knowledge of mental illnesses test (MC-KOMIT)	D. Heroin withdrawal	D. 海洛因戒断	D. 戒除毒瘾	Quit addiction	Cultural comprehensibility
33-item version of the multiple-choice knowledge of mental illnesses test (MC-KOMIT)	B. Impairment in daily functioning	B. 日常功能受损	B. 不能自理	Cannot perform essential daily activities	Cultural comprehensibility

(continued)

Appendix A: Translation of Mental Disorder Terms

Source	English	Forward translation Chinese	Cultural adaptation translation	Backward translation English	Cultural adaptation
33-item version of the multiple-choice knowledge of mental illnesses test (MC-KOMIT)	D1b. A woman sees a therapist weekly to work on her maladaptive patterns of behavior which have repeatedly interfered with relationships and work. When stressed out, she becomes very impulsive, feels empty, thinks of suicide, and makes multiple cuts on her forearms. Which of the following most likely contributed to her problems?	D1b. 一名女性每周都会去看心理医生,以解决她的适应不良行为模式,这些反复出现的行为一再影响了她的人际关系和工作。当压力过大时,她会变得非常冲动,感到空虚,想到自杀,并在前臂上划出多道伤口。以下哪种情况最有可能导致她的问题?	D1b. 一名女性每周都会去看治疗师寻求帮助。因为无法适应工作压力,她的一些反复出现的行为已经干扰到她的工作,以及和其他人的关系。当压力很大时,她会变得非常冲动,感到空虚,想要自杀,在手臂上有多处切口。以下哪一项最有可能导致她出现问题?	A woman sees a therapist weekly for help. Because of her inability to cope with the stress of her job, some of her recurring behaviors have interfered with her work and her relationships with other people. When stressed, she becomes very impulsive, feels empty, wants to kill herself, and has multiple cuts on her arms. Which of the following is most likely to contribute to her problems?	Cultural comprehensibility
33-item version of the multiple-choice knowledge of mental illnesses test (MC-KOMIT)	B. Intrusive thoughts or impulses	B. 侵入性想法或冲动	B. 不由自主、反复出现的想法和冲动	Involuntary, recurring thoughts and impulses	Cultural comprehensibility
33-item version of the multiple-choice knowledge of mental illnesses test (MC-KOMIT)	A. Case managers	A. 案件经理	A. 病例管理员	Managers of medical cases of illness	Cultural comprehensibility

(continued)

(continued)

Source	English	Forward translation Chinese	Cultural adaptation translation	Backward translation English	Cultural adaptation
33-item version of the multiple-choice knowledge of mental illnesses test (MC-KOMIT)	B. Family therapists	B. 家庭治疗师	B. 家庭关系改善治疗师	Therapists for improving family relationships	Cultural relevance
33-item version of the multiple-choice knowledge of mental illnesses test (MC-KOMIT)	B5a. Most people in treatment for depression are treated by which of the following? C. Primary care physicians	C. 初级保健医生	C. 医生	Doctors	Cultural relevance
33-item version of the multiple-choice knowledge of mental illnesses test (MC-KOMIT)	E. The clergy	E. 神职人员	N/A	This concept is not relevant in the Chinese context.	Cultural relevance
33-item version of the multiple-choice knowledge of mental illnesses test (MC-KOMIT)	F4a. Which of the following best describes the treatment approach for developmental disabilities? B. Combination of special supports and services	B. 特殊支持和服务的组合	B. 针对残疾人的支持与服务相结合	Integration of support and services to people with disability	Cultural relevance
33-item version of the multiple-choice knowledge of mental illnesses test (MC-KOMIT)	F4a. Which of the following best describes the treatment approach for developmental disabilities? C. Long-term institutional care	C. 长期机构护理	C. 长期残疾人福利院护理	Long-term institutionalized care for people with disability	Cultural relevance

(continued)

Appendix A: Translation of Mental Disorder Terms

(continued)

Source	English	Forward translation Chinese	Cultural adaptation translation	Backward translation English	Cultural adaptation
33-item version of the multiple-choice knowledge of mental illnesses test (MC-KOMIT)	G5b. A mother and father meet with a mental health professional for three sessions over the course of a month after their 25-year-old son committed suicide. Which of the following is the most likely reason for their meetings? B. To attempt to determine what the warning signs had been	B. 试图确定有哪些警告信号。	B. 试图找出他们儿子自杀的前兆。	Attempting to find out the warning signs of their son's suicide	Cultural comprehensibility
33-item version of the multiple-choice knowledge of mental illnesses test (MC-KOMIT)	H1a. Which of the following is likely a cause of attention-deficit/hyperactivity disorder in children? E. Poor control over classrooms	E. 教室管理不善。	E. 课堂混乱,学生无法专心学习。	Classes are disorganized and students are unable to concentrate.	Cultural comprehensibility
33-item version of the multiple-choice knowledge of mental illnesses test (MC-KOMIT)	J3a. Which of the following is the most common long-term course of dementia?	J3a. 以下哪种情况是最常见的痴呆症长期病程?	J3a. 痴呆症的发展,以下哪种情况最为常见?	Which of the following is most common in the development of dementia?	Cultural comprehensibility
33-item version of the multiple-choice knowledge of mental illnesses test (MC-KOMIT)	A. Improvement	A. 改进	A. 有所改善	Improvement	Cultural comprehensibility

(continued)

Appendix A: Translation of Mental Disorder Terms

(continued)

Source	English	Forward translation Chinese	Cultural adaptation translation	Backward translation English	Cultural adaptation
33-item version of the multiple-choice knowledge of mental illnesses test (MC-KOMIT)	C. Progression	C. 进步	C. 恶化	Deterioriation	Cultural comprehensibility
33-item version of the multiple-choice knowledge of mental illnesses test (MC-KOMIT)	E. Stabilization	E. 稳定化	E. 病情稳定	Medical condition stabilisation	Cultural comprehensibility
33-item version of the multiple-choice knowledge of mental illnesses test (MC-KOMIT)	C2a. Which of the following is a common sign of mania? C. Experiencing repeated flashbacks	C. 反复出现闪回。	C. 头脑中反复出现痛苦的往事和经历。	Painful memories and experiences recur in the mind.	Cultural comprehensibility
33-item version of the multiple-choice knowledge of mental illnesses test (MC-KOMIT)	B. Delirium	B. 病妄	B. 急性意识障碍(一种特定的急性意识模糊状态)	Acute cerebral syndrome (a specific acute state of blurred consciousness)	Cultural acceptability
33-item version of the multiple-choice knowledge of mental illnesses test (MC-KOMIT)	C. Mania	C. 狂躁	C. 极度兴奋(一种伴有情绪高涨的过度反应的状态)	Extreme arousal (a state of overreaction accompanied by heightened emotions)	Cultural acceptability

(continued)

Appendix A: Translation of Mental Disorder Terms

Source	English	Forward translation Chinese	Cultural adaptation translation	Backward translation English	Cultural adaptation
33-item version of the multiple-choice knowledge of mental illnesses test (MC-KOMIT)	E. Pathological lying	E. 病态说谎	E. 非自主性的说谎障碍	Involuntary lying disorder	Cultural acceptability
33-item version of the multiple-choice knowledge of mental illnesses test (MC-KOMIT)	D3a. People who have personality disorders usually have these problems during which of the following life stages? B. After major life events	B. 重大生活事件后。	B. 对人生有重大影响的事情以后。	After events that have a major impact on one's life.	Cultural acceptability
33-item version of the multiple-choice knowledge of mental illnesses test (MC-KOMIT)	E4b. A man has been having episodes of chest pain, hyperventilation, and extreme anxiety during the past few months. He is afraid that he will die of a heart attack during one of these episodes. He has seen several doctors, who assure him that his heart is healthy. He now avoids driving because it seems to trigger these attacks. Which of the following treatments would be most helpful?	E4b. 过去几个月，一名男子出现胸痛、换气过度和极度焦虑的症状。他担心自己会在其中一次发作中死于心脏病。他看过几位医生，他们向他保证他的心脏是健康的。他现在避免开车，因为开车似乎会引发这些袭击。以下哪种治疗最有帮助？	E4b。一名男子几个月来一直胸痛、高通气和极度焦虑的症状。他担心自己会因为这些症状再次发作而死于心脏病。他看了几位医生，医生向他保证他的心脏状况良好。他目前尽量不开车，因为开车似乎会引发这些症状。以下哪种治疗方法最适合他？	The man had been experiencing chest pain, hyperventilation and extreme anxiety for several months. He was worried that he would die of a heart attack due to another episode of these symptoms. He has seen several doctors who have assured him that his heart is in good condition. He currently tries not to drive because driving seems to trigger these symptoms. Which of the following treatments would be most appropriate for him?	Cultural comprehensibility

(continued)

(continued)

Source	English	Forward translation Chinese	Cultural adaptation translation	Backward translation English	Cultural adaptation
33-item version of the multiple-choice knowledge of mental illnesses test (MC-KOMIT)	B. Herbal supplements	B. 草药补充剂	B. 草药保健品	Herbal supplements	Cultural comprehensibility
33-item version of the multiple-choice knowledge of mental illnesses test (MC-KOMIT)	H2a. Which of the following is a common sign of oppositional defiant disorder in childhood?	H2a. 以下哪项是儿童期对立违抗障碍的常见表现?	H2a.以下哪项症状在儿童对立反抗障碍中很常见?	Which of the following symptoms is common in children with oppositional defiant disorder?	Cultural acceptability
Psychiatric scepticism scale	3. The definitions, or criteria for, many current psychiatric disorders leave too much room for opinions and interpretations.	3. 目前许多精神疾病的定义或标准都留下了太多的意见和解释空间。	3. 目前对多精神障碍症的定义和标准还有很多需要完善的地方。	Current definitions and criteria for many mental disorders leave much to be improved.	Cultural comprehensibility
Psychiatric scepticism scale	7. Psychiatry inappropriately excludes other approaches (e.g. alternative medicine) to mental distress.	7. 精神病学不恰当地排除了治疗精神痛苦的其他方法(如替代医学)。	7. 精神病学排除其他治疗各种心理困难的方法(如非西医治疗),这是不恰当的。	It is inappropriate for psychiatry to exclude other treatments for various psychological difficulties (e.g., non-Western treatments).	Cultural acceptability
Psychiatric scepticism scale	14. Psychiatric diagnoses serve to pathologize individuals simply for being different.	14. 精神病学诊断仅仅因为个体的不同而对个体进行病理学分析。	14. 精神病诊断把一些人诊断为有心理疾病的人,而他们只不过和其他人不同而已。	A psychiatric diagnosis diagnoses some people as having a mental illness when they are merely different from others.	Cultural comprehensibility

SPRINGER NATURE

GPSR Compliance

The European Union's (EU) General Product Safety Regulation (GPSR) is a set of rules that requires consumer products to be safe and our obligations to ensure this.

If you have any concerns about our products, you can contact us on ProductSafety@springernature.com

In case Publisher is established outside the EU, the EU authorized representative is:

Springer Nature Customer Service Center GmbH
Europaplatz 3
69115 Heidelberg, Germany

The manufacturer's authorised representative in the EU is Springer Nature Customer Service Centre GmbH, Europaplatz 3, 69115 Heidelberg, Germany. If you have any concerns regarding our products, please contact ProductSafety@springernature.com

Printed and bound by CPI Group (UK) Ltd, Croydon, CR0 4YY

25/03/2026

02078172-0015